Past Futures
—Collected Poems—

By the Same Author

Token and Trace
Metamorphosed from the Adjacent Cold
Leavetakings
Sleeping It Off
Cold's Determinations

Clive Faust

Past Futures

—Collected Poems—

Shearsman Books
in association with Skysill Press

First published in the United Kingdom in 2017 by
Shearsman Books
50 Westons Hill Drive
Emersons Green
BRISTOL
BS16 7DF

Shearsman Books Ltd Registered Office
30–31 St. James Place, Mangotsfield, Bristol BS16 9JB
(this address not for correspondence)

www.shearsman.com

*This edition is published in association
with Skysill Press, Nottingham.*

ISBN 978-1-84861-540-3

Copyright © Clive Faust, 2017.

The right of Clive Faust to be identified as the author of this work has been asserted by him in accordance with the Copyrights, Designs and Patents Act of 1988.
All rights reserved.

ACKNOWLEDGEMENTS

The publisher thanks John Phillips for his assistance
in the preparation of this volume for publication.

The poems assembled here previously appeared in
Token and Trace (Chagford, Devon: Tangent Books, 1980),
Metamorphosed from the Adjacent Cold (Boston, MA: Origin Press, 1980),
Leavetakings (Kyoto: Origin Press, 1986),
Sleeping It Off ([Brattleboro, VT]: Origin Press, 1992), and
Cold's Determinations (Salzburg: University of Salzburg Press, 1996).

Uncollected poems previously appeared in the following magazines:
*Poetry Salzburg Review, Origin (Sixth Series), Tangram,
Damn the Caesars* and *Hassle.*

Contents

Metamorphosed from the Adjacent Cold

Contemplating Mountains in Sung Mist	15
Non-Being or Non-Becoming	16
Without Theodolite	17
In Earnest	18
An Audience	19
Self-Census	20
Near the Park	22
Routines for a Meta-Language above the Snow Line	23
In Answer	25
Lagoons	26
Some Hints	27
Treading the Balance	28
Sequences in Separation	30
A Gift of a Record of Mozart Chamber Music	31
The Vantage	32
Empty at Resting	34
The Movements of Space	36
After Some Sort of Poise	37
Kept-off Sun	39
A Bamboo Flute	40
Life's Short	41
Lasting into Cleanness	42
Expansions in Breath	43
Backway to the Times	44
The Tradition in Australia	47
The Long Expatriation	49
Against Outside-Us	50
Slabs Ajar	52
Metal Fatigues	54
Tensile Strength	56
Survival to any Purpose	57
The One and the Many	59
Remote Education	60

To Tread along the Mean	61
Excavations along the Nile	63
Responsories	65
A Japanese Buddhist Monument	66

Token and Trace

Re-pair	71
The Air in the Well	72
Deliberative Meander near the Great Ocean	73
Accommodation	74
Indifference as Difference	75
Wants: Finite, Infinite	76
Durability	77
Token or Trace	78
Extrusions into a Perspective	80
Wet Night	81
Revanche	83
Light Pools at Night	85
Anxieties	86
"The dusk filters through"	87
Ageing Acceptances	88
Sun-Following	89
A Change Blowing Up	90
Dispossessed	91
The Nurse Carrying My Suitcases	92
The 'Set' of Form	94
The Chinese Scroll	95
Otiose	97
Mantis on Chair	98
Night at Fireworks	99

Addenda to First Two Volumes

Docks and Harbour	103
Working Outside	104
Fishing Tackle	

105

Leavetakings

Midnight Bell at Chion-in	109
Some Comforting in Age	111
To Stop My Thinking with	112
Preparing and Eating an Evening Meal	113
Stamina for Some Other Purpose	115
Water Surface Light	117
From Cars to the Beach and Gulls	119
Failures	121
Keeping it Together	124
Faces in Cold	125
Options	126
Loosed from Music	127
Frost Breath	128
Thinking Unsuccess	129
Solo Concert	130
Worth Living	131
The Presences	132
Oblation Before Entering the Temple	133
Broken Foot	134
With You	135
Recollections	137
Gathering and Dispersal	138
Leavetaking	139

Addendum to *Leavetakings*

Along a Nature Strip	143

Sleeping It Off

Sleeping It Off	147
Mnemonics	149
Doppelgängers	150
Possessive Adjectives	151
Shifting Fortifications	152
Insecticide	153
The R.S.L. Reunion	154
In Concern	156

Recognitions	157
Jay-Walking	158
Top Forty or Whatever They're called Now	159
The Japanese Buddhist Cemetery	160
After Shutting the Gates	161
Carrying On	163
The Tarot Reading	165
Unalienated	167
Loading Beer Barrels	169
The Length of the Spell—Three Episodes	170
The Habits	172
After the Equinox	173
The Salivation	174
The Revenant	176
Park Near Evening	178
On Acceptance	180
Immaturations	181
Visiting Hours	182
The Journey	184
Work at the Sawmill and After	185

Addendum to *Sleeping it Off*

The Bogongs	189
Muscle Tone	191
Customary Relationship	192
From "Individual Needs"	193
Into Night	194
Moving Off	195
Cha-no-yu	196
An Open Air Fight	197
Games' Venues	199
On the Money	201
The Church Dance	203
Reworkings, Inactivities	205
Anaesthetic	207
Roll Call (Role Call)	208
Rhythms to Counter-Rhythms	210

Restoration	211
The Feast of Or-Bon (pron. "Or-Bon")…	214

The 'Late' Section from *Cold's Determinations*

Skywriting	219
Below the Waterline	220
The Life's Work	221
On Bivouac	222
Ex Cathedra in Bourges Cathedral	224
The Effort	226
Last Watering Place	228
Double or Quits	232
The Recollection	234
Systole	235
Family Continuities and Discontinuities	236
Mechanical Engineering Show at the Exhibition Building	240
Uses of Iron	241
Hortus Conclusus	242
Retreat in the Jesuit Seminary	243
Winter Temple	245
Down from the Mountains	247
Childhood Illness	248
Legal Action	251
Storage Space	255
Off and Out	257
The Wreath	258
Past Futures	259
Cold's Determinations	262

Postscript

A Need for Manipulation	267
Post-Obituaries	268
The Avenue of Trees	269
Match Points	270
Long Division	271
A Day Off	272

A Buzz out of the Regiment	273
Individuals in Collectivity	274
Returnings	275
Low Tide	276
Burning of the Great Dai on Daimonji	278
Training Route	279
Hygiene	280
Some Sense from it	281
Manipulative Crafts	282
The Fifty Year Reunion	283
Marist Brothers' College Bendigo	284
Serial Modes	286
Substantial Identities	287
Nobody Home	288
Exchange between Acceptance and Recalcitrance	289
Gesticulating with Whalen in the Open Air	290
Ave atque vale, Owen Faust	291
Dusk from Inside the House	293
Collapsions	294
Corollary to a Theme of Corman	295
Out to Do Some Shopping	296
Route to the Abattoirs	297
Syllables to and from Cid	298
Electric Razor's Somatics	300
Closed Discussions with Cid	301
Foyer	302

Preface

Off-putting to think about the relationship between my life and my poetry, and how complicated either of the pair would be, let alone their relationship.

I have attempted to fit narratives to both of them, and both of them admit narratives, yet these histories occur by happenchance, mostly, even when one has arranged events in advance, while other stories, and self-constructed un-stories, could well have evolved, and jostled with each other and me, as definitive for either self or the verse.

As there is nothing finalised about this me, even its past phases, nor about the poetry—for that's been allowed to wander loose, and I have avoided drafting it into military service, or any personal or social causes—even ones I myself have been committed to.

For poetry is not a communal activity, yet it is engendered by people—and each of them has a particular communal base. While one is indebted to that base for being human at all—and it is only humans who write poetry. Even though poetry is not in itself a human activity.

So, as ever, I thank my friends, my relatives, my acquaintances, even my enemies, for "helping" form the necessary pre-condition for any writing of poetry, and having endured the avoidance of them that any writing of poetry usually entails. As a fellow human, I feel sorry for them, and even at times sorry for the human in myself; but the vocation of poetry is absolute and, to such people (and sometimes to myself) unfair.

So yet again I want to thank my dead friends: Ian Watson, my mother, my father, my brother, a favourite aunt, Thelma and her husband Chas, aunt Marea, my maternal grandfather, Paddie McVay, Trevor Artingstall (let's hope not dead), Brother James Nash, and unfortunately a host of others.

While still living would be Di Sewell, Michael Hallpike, Sally Holmes, Roger Sworder, Cheryl Russell, Maurice Nestor, Tara Debrodt, Fr. Leo. Hynes, Anthony Hannan, Ron Stewart, Dietrich Faust, Leopold Faust, Konrad Faust, Siegfried Faust and Ros Webster.

Others—and perhaps some of them have not lasted the journey—and I understand that for I have not always lasted the journey myself. But I remember them, and with at the very least residual fondness.

More than other friends have been active in ensuring I could be published. And John Phillips, Jan Bender and Kris Hemensley come immediately to mind, as well as Cid Corman, thirteen years dead. All of them very fine poets. Without these longstanding friends I would have remained unheard.

And finally, an acknowledgment of the setting, in time and place. I've often wondered if mine were the proper environs for poetry, with their isolation, both interior and exterior, and their unfinality. Probably a stupid question, but they'll do, it'll do—or, it has done. The local habitation and a name is the somewhere without which poetry would be nowhere at all, nor be the some place you'd need to go to it from.

Clive Faust

METAMORPHOSED
FROM THE ADJACENT COLD

Contemplating Mountains in Sung Mist

In
    comparable
alone, last
gift of the one-and-many,
wherever we're left to feel to that
                              after
words
      other

human contact
some contact
             would've filled

us in. Sumiye dried
onto rice paper, to loan-bulked mountain
against white mist.
                The

spread of inkbrush, strands,
into single pine needles, spaces

within anything that we know,
out to nothing still uninked in.

Non-Being or Non-Becoming

The Essence of God
is irremovable
from us;
likewise we have it

only as a cure
for one ill. The Friend

we would talk to, *do* something with—
vacuum floors,
walk paths along near
hedges of red hollyhock down

the garden—is a dark
intruder there that's meant
for intruders. As we are—
unfounded. As it is—
reducing us to a what-is-not,
unknown
number

to what is wanted.

Without Theodolite

Require
space, no other physical
property.
Glass squares
ruled up

in the dark—
              a geometry
over contours
              ideally flat.

To transpose and forget
what needed no transposing
for our purpose. Steams, off breath,
through stone of openwork, latticework, set
into rib sides,
              stone clarity.

To forget system and structure

while we're getting it clear

Day, clear, motionless air.
Cool—you move through it,
without hindrance, as the given, jerk
clump-foot on the worn flagged site.

In Earnest

Who's to tell
me what to do
about it,
anything?
        Days

pass by like nights—
of recuperation and rest
for nothing.
          Nights come
with strain of a purpose
dissatisfied.
       Bring
            me

rest from myself
in act as my mode—
as *anything*. Belief

that what's t' be done
is to be done. Content,
asking a question—

as what I know only too well.

An Audience

                Would there be Last
Judgement upon us, let sink in
just what we are, to know we always have been,
uncalled for and unasked— since a First Judgment
the getting here at all? No progress
after that, never, unforced
to whatever denomination, as a necessity
of the Principium Individuationis: as if
ourselves, when *from* ourselves: blocked in,
blocked out time space, with a sense
the both could be anywhere—
                                in audience
of ourselves.

                Don't know
what's the inevitable, at casual
of the makeshift, after the seven years is it?
of the phases of the moon in our body chemistry,
darks sandbanked under brightness. After, a fall
should be Inevitable, still impermanent.

While I squat here, hunched shoulders beside a heater,
metamorphosed by it
                            out of the adjacent cold.

Self-Census

Details of a life? Not
for now. *As* for now: cold,
skin in, chafed
at the bracing.
                The twisted wire-loop
fence—is't gate?—I
felt it, hand slipped
with glaze t' corrugations near
the rust, the paintless.

After
     cold
would be violet nights
not so dark
blue.
          I
hear
     my
          footsteps
close but someone else's
a ricochet half-a-step ahead
on the path. Once, twice, thrice and three
kittens: the witch went into the wood.
Header up,
         almost into
door—old, panels,
at an angle against corner.

Step!
     Unfroze.
Runnels switching slipping across
but ground still
            hard, tamped
cold,

black.
There's

freeze round way back of wall's
edge, back into next week,
some-
        where-
               else.
When's?
I

should be more tem-
               porary;
scarish, and unscared.

Near the Park

Dogs
care together slowly,
sniff
off each other dis-
　　　　　　gusted
not with the scent but what it *means*
to smell of sickness just
　　　　　　　like that; se-
duction's preliminary in-
duction, be-fore dreams
of saliva. Yet
their hungers are what disgust us, peri-
stalsis mucus-wet, might be
our bellies, pricks, testes,
like water bags on wet poles. The dogs
are doggy themselves, slap tongues around
like water off wet washing.

And trot off for a piss in the park.

Routines for a Meta-Language
above the Snow Line

I wring my clothes in a handwash, put my hand to it—
obliterativeness.
                    From untwists of washing
to turn through a wringer by hand,
with smudge off inky fingers from an italic
pen.
       The kinaesthetic exhaustion—
forearms, wrists, wet fingers. Mind

comes up nap-raised from a wringer,
curled upwards pressed folds in clothing.
I
know I know:

as Peace.

What the workman
should be doing, drudge
dredge rhythm
               unthought
                                  buoyant. In-
evitable the day

draws in draws down in a window framing air:
washroom basilica, closed vault,
apse of blue walls. I nose effectiveness

from something I half-remember: not to pursue
my memories further, the distances're too far.
A rose chill fades, darkens, mid-angelus,
densens into colours, texture of stalactites
caves at midday. Meditation ruffles itself against the lie
of hair/fur. Thought bleached to a sun—

blonde body divested of royal
clothing;
is it necessary to think?
      We enter
in upon night, shut heavy front door, bolt it.

Move over to hearth fire's projecting angle,
cold at our backs,
      the contrast to our security,
a tree shadow still out there on the snow clearing
tramped in—but now it's after.
Lit by gas's smoulder, 'coals',
thought
hovers high with a powder glitter star
in the Christmas decorations. Sound sleep
should be so compensation in cold bed
warmed up by us, want
      dozes off inert
till after dawn, and the spread pulse-cold
of a summer mountain sunrise, expanding
into indolence clarity after the streak-cloud
narrowness at first grey light.

In Answer

      The function
of stupidity: not the economy
so much, the numbing it out;
but estimate of the ungiving in matter, solid.

Lack in gaiety
      from the door you blunder against
when you forget
      or treat it as function
for shutting-out cold, for opening-in air.

              Answering to gravity
of self— body's sense
of Id-self among objects,
      you
who are not itself, but essence, un-

sonorous off the thickness of it, the
clumsiness of it afoot, blunder-
adroit against incomprehensible
worldly, tactful to its heavy tact,
in an individual among the undivideds.

Lagoons

        The Terrible
floated over on principles like gondolas,
cooling with their wash the sun-hot stones
in splashed sound.

        To get together
with humans to ride it out, stirred up
water, the para-
                sympathetic
systems. Subtle solutions.
                      Deli-
                        cacies
in reflection. The city quelled,
quelled.
        The get-togethering
of the media dead
                foreshortened
at angles—oil slick
over waver of iridescent coral
towers.
The bump of water.

Some Hints

                I thought of how
elusive behaviour is to any reading,
even when we have one, put up close
together with one use. She spoke, grinned,
terminated a friendship that hadn't started,
hinting it could start now. Easy
you gestalt the must-have-beens. Both's
motives fall in place,
                      both's. Then

did she *love* me,
            I her,
                    had we some darker
substitute for such 'love'?
                          What consequence anyhow
if she'd not said just how much she was
mad crazy for me, when I said nothing?

'Years will show what that meant.'
                            Sentiments
after youth, of youth coulda believed,
when we know how much loss there is,
                        how little
we miss finally what's lost.
                    I come in now;
close the flywire door, bang it to wedge it shut.
The crickets're flicking chirrup over the dust.
Out through the wire mesh it's the half-dark.

Treading the Balance

I've yet to be convinced
it could've meant much. She kept herself
too guarded, used it
too conveniently against life together,
if only for a tine—at
edge for us to be off-balance
on, as democracy
within the bedroom. Off-

balance I know.
And live there.
Still.
No *needs*'ve made it.

Inspection was hers,
for her. I remember, though,
fun, pricks of pride, the bum
up the steep steps, wooden—
was just a ladder—jerk-
roll in the bum-bumps at
side-weighs.
          Insulted?

Embarrassed: not knowing,
up, how the bum looked
from nether post, what
'we' would've thought of it.
              Seems

not a long tine back, but
final. Place
might have been, after was
demolished. Mortar dust

'd have settled, powdered stairs
to a 'recess' viz. loft
of a bedroom. I

do not feel human
towards her, who was cold
with unwelcome for whatever
that I was. I was nothing

human, her fear
of a violence, no violence,
ununderstandable as a peace
out of the near-nothing still mine.

Sequences in Separation

We broke up before that.
                        To 'sojourn'.
The sojourn was final. With a new year
I met my 'own love'. And the sequence
of that 'engraved itself on my character'.
And I never got over it—
I guess.
And the events,
natural logic,
podded out, down into the ground,
as in empathy, as to growth vegetation, as a 'character'.

I can't place the years now. It doesn't seem
to matter which
                    could have been first or second:
the premonition of love during marriage
to someone else which h'd caused it break up—
for a someone that I *could* love, immaterial
if the someone has materialised,
                              when you *had*.

At solitude without competitors. I can't place
the dates—it wouldn't have a knack-
of revealing them as causes, either final
or material.
        The fingers

untangling fishing lines with dumb skill—

out of the intricacies of geometry—
from snarls,
            if they've felt where to start.

A Gift of a Record of Mozart Chamber Music

to Sally

A word or two
more or less
than I meant to—

the *same*—and same consequence

to follow from the surfeit—
more, or less;
           I wish to give

out what you'll 've taken,
as Anyhow is to give it,
prodigally—that is, Absolutely

enough. Why bring it so
to my attention that I love you;
that I love you at a love
too generous for me?—verb
and noun. Such presents

of each out to the other,

as other. Too meagre!
                    Too *immoderato*,
the notes of a Mozart quintet,
the *in memoriams*, the black
niello work burnt on,
                  and love
in gifts since we
           fear to receive it.

The Vantage

        Back here:
some years gone between us
                  between
others no doubt, but who
knows them, what they still
are to each other—in
themselves.
      Alone
            just
the pair of us, where
they make vantage of us. Some

years from where we should've gone,
but didn't. Any terminus

that seemed to allow,
            as if
some end to what we were, would've been
only if we had wanted it,
            had been
the sort of people to have wanted it.

                The Byrd
mass creates shafts
between light,
        graduates
at ritornello floated to
a ceiling.

     Wings of the Wilton
Diptych arc centre
from feather points on circumference
down shafts to centre, or close,
at gap around in which they never
touch.

        Shines off feathers
blurred over blues
of the angels' cote-hardies in Richard's
livery within radii
of the dance to their points.

                        No

regrets about the passing
of youth or of the young friends
who are all one of them old. Stone
ground of the cathedral
earths it

longer to earth
than earth does. The vaults thrust
up down to calibrate
stillness that is contained
within it at a space empty
to their heights.

Empty at Resting

What was
once God
to me

is Godless.
          Rain drenching
the ground, feet. Will have left off
later, come night.

Night—cold, clear;
wind, wavering off stars (shred-clouds
taking them out). Me
not so much breathless as
unwanted here. Life

leaves blanks—
               the knowledge
as to where *anything* might be,
or we are.
         God still

not so much unwelcome as
unwanted.
         We make
              small

talk about kindness
in general, but do it *only*
in particular…

(and should).
          Visit ends
to old patients' home
a little before time,

leaving
each there to himself.
                        Pretence
                                        's
gone with the visit.

(That much to say for it.)
                        You
remember shake hands—
a form of formality.
                        (How
it was done—still is.)
                        Some
bell rings
        dusk-
angelus
        as a practice
carillon.

            Bells
are mathematical and beautiful.
                        Night

rises like air
before sunrise;
            clear,
is empty of God,
and of yourself.

The Movements of Space

Stepping over
    onto gravel
    to avoid cars
        that would not avoid
        me,

      Insteps short
   of a full step. Need

to be overtaken by someone
unscheduled t' pick me up.

Path close to paddock edge
through puddle under fence,
well below the build up
of roadside.

    Cloud massif
above shred vapours
    lower
       spread
on wind towards us darkening
at the gaps.
   The

divergent movements
of space,
layers
across paddock
    in total wind.
       Objects

as if nothing to be known.

After Some Sort of Poise

                The tremblings,
the rub-scrapes of a front-end loader,
a power shovel—not just yours,
the *body's* inferences from it
in lymphatic depths.

Shouts
return, bouts of boys' wit,
lifted in trajectories—
yonnies through the air—
subsidence at subsistence.
                      Light
clear,
        down from grey cloud—
suspensions of light, in air

under it, white-grey
vapours beneath darks
shifting across, all, still
moving.

      Absorbed

light on vests
in orange phosphorescence of
the roadworkers—
             like paint
on weatherboards of the New Australian
housefronts, up to unhipped roofs
on gables below.
             The place is

so *old*, that once seemed
my parents' age—as … 'adult'. Birds

chatter quirrip preep
on the bird bath like a font
or the stone *lavatorium*
                                            used
for washing monks' hands, same

(the cement) as my parents' day. We'll
tell the children
whatever they'll want to know
if they'd care to listen. Past
interpreted as history,
like the one they would tell us about
themselves, if we could live it with them,
could stay till then. The workmen

mend roads. Our understanding
comes with the diesel vibrate
scrape.

Kept-Off Sun

No people,
or groups—
              here.

Except in unpeopled light.
                      For others

'buried in obscurity
like ourselves', for ourselves,
                      women

have been taught to wear shawls, black
head covering across black hair
to keep the sunlight off it, unearthly
wettings in black sheen.

                 Where is
the world gone that we would've come for?
            Just gone.

    As if
what is not

as if

whatever
is

still to come.

A Bamboo Flute

Once happy
          to be doubly
miserable to have been once happy:
the dialectic, the teaching.

The pain of presence,
Autumn of absence—trees
above head height
shaping drift wind
to the cut of pared leaves, wind
whittled to windlessness.

Seen;
      forgotten,
except as mnemonic,
its ghost past, past
of what we won't remember—
a here-now,
          absence
in this place, as no
where else—the shakuhachi,
 ghost music imitating
the wind we don't remember.

Life's Short

(A balloon—lift of warm air—

floats from the lead string,
that moored it to the ground…

something for it to elevate itself
from off.)
          Why should
we be happy—even with ourselves?
There is no despair, worry.
We learn nothing from our happiness.

Lasting into Cleanness

The fear—sharp,
ready at the quiet—
where it has taken over.

You
get easy with it.

            With space

indoors—
      silence
come
     touchable like a windbell, wind

twisting card with clapper tinkled
on it—
     foretaste
of peace, cleanness.
The Chinese

censer on the table, smoke
curling, backing off,

against nothing
              spaced through slot curves

on the grid.

Expansions in Breath

What is there
to explain now?
                Nothing
                They don't need it.
(Neither do I.)
Except see if it's true,
what it looks like still, where
we've come to together.
                The primitive

phrases made positive,
as still possible.
                The Rosary
said by myself—
            wood

beads mark hands
like a dogma, rest
upon thumb webs, tendons
at back of hand, straight

links into continuity
down loop's bend to the other side
below.

        The breath spaces
within the litany, chants
within darkness among candles, as

remote as the substance
of holes within the Trinity
out into the
blank full, lit
singing we'd have come from.

Backway to the Times

Don't care if the arguments
happened
        just as he told them
whether
the boss'd called him Paddy or Mr McVay
not the
'McVay' as if a servant.

        Wet
wheels on the upper class
hansoms
        from a hydrant
on his horse-drawn
        street cleaner's
water wagon that he'd pedalled jets
from.
    "In my rights. And
were they annoyed!"

        Formed

an 'image' of himself well
in these talks: tough, strong back,
head body cocked to it,
mother wit, not too many
tumbles—though could imitate
his own embarrassed face well
when he told of one.
        Gone

like the land of the Mughal tombs, left
in these grandfathers of a memory.
        I can't

snuff sense of this world
from anthropology, suchlike.
                              Yet it
'seemed' natural, the legendary,
just as he told it. People

boiled billies for tea, tealeaves
floating next t' gumtwigs, taste
tin of billy drinking. And people

talking talking, opinionated,
'spinning yarns'.
               After

was supper, dancing to accordion,
Pride of Erin, waltz, viz
the throopenny bit circulars, on
till dawn and into another day's
work, its dancing after.
                    I

could feel what he meant
from a beginning to my own labourer's
back, sinews tightened with shoulders
that'd learnt t' bear a load.
And the wit?
                   Yes I knew it

myself—but this was physical:
not bulk but speed, to show you were
too swift for them in movement, not
in movement,
                but speech. Have seen him

front of his oiled furniture,
dressing table with round two-sided
shaving mirror, one side of it

magnifying, rasp
at neck with cutthroat under moustache
to take a lather off,
                      under

eyes, bleach-whitened, sunk
with age to undefining over
cropped moustache reflected back
within an oak frame. Gone—

like the Incas or the Aztecs—out
onto the spaces of the millennia.

Or the land of the Mughal tombs. The gaslight
in the streets of Edwardian London.
Or the childhood in which you read about them,

heard him,
while turning logs
                      with the black-painted

iron

       tongs,

          buffeting off on the fender,

the smouldering char and ash.

The Tradition in Australia

                Arguing
with another group of oldies. Woman
banged door against my car—no
apologies, no 'need' for it. Their

property'd be as inviolable
as their hatred viz. of any of us
           'young',
               snip-handbagged
into memories of those who'd done them in
suspicions
of diddling t' come.
               Loose

clothing, *gone* loose (didn't
know he'd shrink) down to
trouser cuffs, lolling, at lean,
on creases outwards. Glasses, the glass
a wall already scaled,

another wall behind, flat
tilted back of bald head, jugged
ears off tufts, their handles unslicked

down for someone else
t' lift.
        Debris

over from some time back. Cartons
at rear of the supermarket, us 'young people'
moving silently like the automatic
doors between them

and what would be going on.

As those who have dispossessed you
from common property, arguing outside, too
confused to refuse the shock.

The Long Expatriation

You said: here I am back at this dump
to yourself. You thought you'd exorcise it so
to itself. The place incorrigible with
your
      self—and then without it? Incorrigible's

the answer—stupid thought. Hot beach head,
sand dried loose by the Aussie sun.
You under, packed to the Past Tense, number none.

And number none's not nothing? At the end
will be none to liberate us from it: single,
but free and devastated by it, in

ourselves as in our memory after. Ports stirred
from a wind straight off the harbour, flapped
strained flags—ours or someone else's?

Against Outside-Us

               I remember
my mother down on her knees
with a scrubbing brush. Wait till the floor's
dry: don't bring mud in.
I had.

       Standing up bent
now long after accident
to her head
           (the brain operation
to 'relieve pressure')
               "People've been
so *good* to me."
           Doubled up
as if knife in stomach still working way
out through her back.

               Catches
the gist, looks up—
still got her half-wits about her
(me)—swaps rules,
if she needs for a defeat. "Come on (this
not to me thank God),
give us a little smile."

            Back
               'home'
by myself at my place, pace, We search out
for anyone who'll come our way—
whether or not they've been asked—
some part of our living/dying;
yet *all*—it would not be their journey.
                       Most

are as we are ourselves, unmovable—
but the *thing* moves, from us with us
in us at its place.
     Blinds

drawn to keep upholstered couch,
armchair, the raised pile design,
from fading.
    Dust's down
in a slant
   floats out light's cuts
at the side of blinds. From late afternoon
half-summer still.
     Dust, caught in hair,
rolls off like fluff-kapok
from linolcum to its edges.
And you settle down
   to think,

in the house
in the dust.

Slabs Ajar

The ancients believed
                          their ghosts should be appeased
against malignity.
            Why

should they give us peace?—they were not

buried in beatitude.

Interred.
Christian rites.
Death ceremonies.

To *sleep*.
         As
            still

ageing with us.

Not
so visible from externals,
traceable
at weathering to a year or so;
but
in notions
of just how old we are,
diseased
discomfort,
lesions
we feel whether they bury us of them
or not.
        It lays

quiet as fat around
the nerves:
in a presence, in a
pre-sense of them there—

the negligence in guilt
that we have learned to live with,
without their memories or, long term,
with their replacement.

Metal Fatigues

Gone deaf or deafish, half-deaf, half-
alive—as they have it—
filter
revs and diesels in
of unsure rustle, warble;
and as deaf-in-the-head, abs-
tract to a pre-stressed
iron skull,
dumb—as the decibels speak through it.

'Nullity is not enough' 's
too much!
Alive
in-
quisitored with the Particular—Being
in un-becoming. Cadence,
at post-coital fatigues of young lovers,
as lusters—
blood globes lit by electric candles, throat
spasm swallow in blackbird's cocked-out spill.

                                        Null,
you walk the limits trodden with sodden oak
leaves still part-crackling after lying sodden.
                                        Transports compress
air in the streets with you,
through, through gears, to immovable-as-an-object,
which is irresistible forces as they converge
at futures junk-arrested.

Like blistered paint,

like rust, such

'things' in your head, such
unrenewabling off material, such
im-material,
free
of analogy, of the Nothing, its
own symmetry—shapeless in-
                    ex-
                        haustible selves, a-
toning,
        at slits in board fence,
quarries
far down off the pavement,

a treble whistle distance to stopped-off workmen.

Tensile Strength

Dried butterfly wings
caught, clapping hands,
on spiderweb at slant roof
to a hangar, acute pitch,
suspension frame
                  holding down skein.

Vaulted in high,

off openwork as mesh,
but kingposts of steel,
girders.

A butterfly cannot fall front there,

or flutter.

Survival to Any Purpose

                    Army
huts, the corrugated iron roof,
faint smear of rust,
unpainted from some time back,
at—period of occupants
who would have moved on,
out from any settlement.

                           Winds

across a district of playing fields,
no boundaries,
                 just closer croppings
of grass. Signs bent,

curved to off-direction,
by a wind everywhere without direction.
                                After

the period of the post-war
years
they stayed there,
not much more dilapidated
than when washing was all around them, nailed
string, a woman transient,
wiping hair off her face with wet
hands,
        the three kids around her, near
window frame, gaps in panes
                           holding
old hut air in, keeping

gusts out.
Life

lived there in the present
as in the unmemorable—
a history that didn't take,
like these huts of an old camp,
we remember that someone had lived in, with us young.

When we might as well 've been anywhere.

The One and the Many

"Give us
a setting again."

Cars move round corners crui-

sing out to avoid you
both ways. You get used to it,
learn cautions without number—
in the damps of days, nights.

You, me—a one-and-many—

someone's afraid

Remote Education

We tour always for uncertainty
'there',
beyond—'come back';

                    catching

the pasts in our breath, wherever
this is, or when, say
home time,
homelessness embracing;

                deliberate

over whether we could return—

ever—

to the Alexandria of the Ptolemies
                                to archaeo-
Logos of its centre

                after

we've laid down tools, cleaned
stone dust from our hands, scraped
grease off
in the rites of purification—
in the Hall of us

to mingle, last, with the Great Ones of Abydos.

To Tread along the Mean

The certainty of it's gone.

Not gone far, it's just a little way off.

Somehow your time is reckonable.
                                       Things

happen all right,
                    to the same you.

No one's different.
                    To find
a temple on massive pole-

piers on a Kyoto hillside housing
a thousand-year-old Kannon Bosatsu
they clap torch-candles near to in its chamber every
thirty three years once only—
and you've seen it (chalk it up).
You didn't
know there was such a temple within yourself,
nor what this showed some about you.
                                     Anything
you don't know now you don't want t' know;
                                         dis-
remember you wanted be, do anything else.

        * * *

The streets're full of cars not of people.
Relax we're in a vehicle. They'll bring takeaways
from the corner—chicken, fish,
both with chips. The taste should spoil
talk, but we know what talk is—

thank God it's spoilt. We know how much
we want *any* of it. Tissues there?
To wipe hands off till clean from oil, fat,
feel things
as a thermostat.

Since it seems—
come to the end of it:
into space not filled up with yourself,

that you were meant to fill.

Excavations along the Nile

Unusable the Past? Well

why do we go to them?—

as we go to our loves
$\qquad$ to tell us we

are worth something

anyhow—we know anyhow
we're not.
$\qquad$ Immobile,

as populace with one face—*if* smiling—answers,

re-
$\quad$ tracting Kouros weight onto back foot

into Tris-magistral stone of what we could guess we are—couldn't tell.
$\quad$ They wait
$\qquad$ speaking *lingua*

franca of the diggings to foreigners

as if to kinsmen.
$\qquad$ They take it,
$\qquad\qquad$ they give it back, dialect

imposition—like the Grecian expressions
upon the stelae, photo-graphic
after two thousand years
of youth, ex-

humed from the workings of Alexandrian
antiquity—
          whose span of life's our *only*
antiquity.
      Yet
they *did* things,
          however they talked
          (in hieroglyphics?),
just as we do, with similar purposes—
          amour-propre,
          love—
          who understand them—
to reduce such things to us.
          Or don't we do

similar things?
          We hope we do.
          We need to.

Did they hope?
Did they have need to?
          The Past

is
for suppression of this relationship

into itself.

Responsories

You must remember what I told you: remember
to keep the talk going, anyhow.
For neither of us's substantial as the talk.

I heard your
comments on the Schoolmen, dis-
putations within a church.
Echoes
double-bounce
off side-walls
walled corners.
Not
to sermon or response. Out of earshot—
if there's anyone to hear within a church.
Responsories. Who 'm I—anyone to speak?
With stones quoined in corner for the silences.

A Japanese Buddhist Monument for the Enlightenment of All the Dead from the Last World War

Glare-gravel
below grease-grime
concrete, the
        'stone'
of the monument. Triangular
onto its base, Kannon—robed
curved sides
        settling
down on concrete particular. Grey
rain stains, acid—
elements don't penetrate

into sealed form
of image through

porosity.

        Still— …
it gives peace.
        Smoke
from an incense I can't smell—
must be there:
        cave-temple
inside robe
        (where iron rods
strut the Bodhisattva
with scaffolding)
        as baldacchino
to drape its own shrine,

Stain on it? Rust?

Incense—

that has fumigated, blessed it,
suspensions of powder
into stalns down rain. The

Dharma has no laws
but breaks them
                breaks them

into laws to be broken,
if only by us,
who piece it to comprehend it.
                        Twist
onto one dropped
              foot
to weight onto
              spine, leg,
at propped steps
              from slipping 'm
too old for.
        Clay
lump, budged, shifts firm
among grey clouds, dries out
heavier than it was. As

the one last to go, stone
steps off the gravel,
                I

clop foot

through woods down

into the gusts of Spring.

TOKEN AND TRACE

Re-pair

Wanted, the truth to be finite and end,
the end to be endless.

Impossible—we have it
as it has always been,
now.

There's a crease of rust across car
where I scratched it. The rain since, falling
several days. Rust dries
like fine powder.
     T' stop
things that start with the rust, with
a rest from labour—

a whole lifetime
updating renovation!

     Choose slow:
inept for a life period,
or work to make it livable, re-

stored. The damp rot
is coming up to meet books not
their contents
where

this is forgotten.

The Air in Well

Every denial has its depth,

denial against;
                nothing

at bottom.

Suspended

well bucket—
hung with it
lowered with it,
no other

depth into once-upon-a-time's
youth. Different age. We
say we are the same.
                Different
words, things themselves different.
Storage amour, dunked in well,
half out of water—
visor split across where it could have

talked—
        as if none
'd understood.
                The bucket

takes weight
as it leaves water,
through air down well

stilled in the long immersion.

Deliberative Meander near the Great Ocean

                      Disencumbered,
a raw wind blows through
and around legs, flapping overcoat.

On the beach I bunch neck stiff
into buttoned flap.

                  The waves near
the jetty's rime-froth slap-
roll. I do not need,
want anyone else particularly whether 'm

meant to or not.

Dry ocean
          scrub brushes
evergreen, back-move roll-
balance. Why should
it be otherwise?

               Dig

                  up

                        sand holes
with the feet, feet *doing* something—

sand lag,
        quantities,
shape lacking out of holes—
in boot toes,
              wet.
Wet sort of freshness. Parti-
cularity's part-raised
and quashed. What

are you doing here, brother?

Accommodation

They get
some understanding going
for sex in the pavilion after,
on plank floors.
                The what

not known too closely
but understood if the effect
not known too closely.

                      God
it is a drab activity—joy
raised up like a sweat, no

truth separate
at rest from
commerce, com-
mingling.
                Her human

smell is uncomfortable,
ours only comfortable
as our body is, the comfort is
its own not ours.
                  Love

demands all it can,
takes what it must, not too
close to the bone, to the
skin it strokes
sweating as in a vision.

Indifference as Difference

Where the hurt is is the indifference
to the hurt
or to the indifference that's t' come of it
eventually.

        Aetiology
is to uncover this metastasis into indifference.
And I wish it would cause you
no pain; but the cuts
are in human meat,
therefore I want you
to *feel* it,
        as I have felt
you in-
human, throbbing
under anaesthesis
            like cement mixer
under the glare sweats
of pain-sleep
        till you come out of them.

Wants: Finite, Infinite

We do not believe
but *know* it—hang
out of it in disposition:
as only character that we have—
as has us for possession.

The knowledge is what we'd hoped for,
assurance
apart at inarticulateness we would fuse
into unknown finalities,
                              into
peace,
       and yet we are not
*un*happy—beyond hope
of beauty for ever.
                    Should

allow torment
enter
wherever it wants to.
                    Ask
to comprehend

there is nothing beyond peace—

except ends,
                    if we could bear them in the pattern.

Durability

In the damp
              stone darknesses
the lantern sways some light.
Re-
     deem
mor-
       tality.
The
Distances
Close for ever.

Token or Trace

To give it close attention
along infinite lines of perspective
upon forgetfulness.
                      To set it
down where our ancestors congregated with Gods
in local staved churches,
                            cross upreared,
backing wooden against heaven
off dolphin gables,
                    protest
at earth's instability, clumsiness.
                                To lift it
before replacing on altar cloth, deposition
of a monstrance laid flatly. To exit porch
before *ite missa est*. Sharp breather
in profanity like the Hall at Versailles.

Heat waves
                disturb the precinct trees
                                    upwards.
                                                Recall

of something we never understood
then—could we understand it now?
Never, probably. Double-exposures,
branch tanglings blanched
on brightness.
                    I want home—
no matter how vacated of people—
                      just self,
to understand such. Come down to the front gate—
you're still unfriendly?—
                          decide
which of us is to be leaving.

Home's switched off, with dawn—
                              displacing

darkness from the hill

to the hot morning.

Extrusions into a Perspective

White
square, paving concrete,
porches breaking in with
intense shadow onto
piazza air.

       Thought

flaked out—dog
asleep—ears fit back
in head. Light/heat accepted

easily,

stupidly—

sweated into coolness.

                You have
the animal to crawl back into;
the mineral—under refined heat—

is crystal against the dark porch.

Wet Night

                The light
crackling in small gravel, for-
tuitous order. Pellucidity's
split up into pieces—stone?
Donna nobis pacem.

Under the wet gravel—
Nothing. Bits rest
on this, each other. Droplets
tilt-drizzle
through arc-mist.
Arc lamp high, pitch
mutation above it,
                configured,

unsettled—and free. Tight,
direction to rain, loose,
crinkle in the light gravel,
slanting from me out of
itself.
      The wind howls of

something inhuman,

This not inhuman
enough.
        Whistle, water pipes
unlaid out by fence, open
piping.
        I can't put
it all together

except through
harmonics in the nerves.

Pipes
 clear,
winds
 in courtyard, seepage,
air between buildings.

Revanche

Flashing blue light—
mudguard metal-cutting a curve to it—swivelling
slower than the road,
                    pivotal
and still down
                into the valley highway,
                        phosphor
torch flares jabbed, gravel, by police
in the approach to it leading up.
                            Tarpaulin covering something
contracted under near parapet of the bridge

cracked outwards.
                Better

I cut back across country.

Some time before it's cleared,

though
        tow-trucks should clear it,
eventually.

        Car
rusty .... Pool, oil? blood?
with it.
        Hope

she notices any difference
if there *is* any. Grant
rest to it—from pew backs
of a mortuary chapel. Had gone out

not blinded by a full moon
but by headlights—

though there *was* a full moon—rammed in
through concrete of parapet
of the bridge, metals recoiling, onto

lurch flight to drag reeds
in shallows of the river.

Light and Dark Pools at Night

                    The premonitions,
the tremorings of the Romantic movement.
                                    What

do we have a disaster
from?

        Under
arc lamp bent over
                    flapping
rocked pools of light-slop—flexible
desk-lamp-type arm,
                    watch
carefully: police car
with questionings from a rolled down
door window—out of my gust-tugged-at,
flap-unzipped
            unknowing.
                        Is

a mood only—thing's so med-
iocritous—to pull you through

to life to question whether
it should connect with love.
                        Slipstream

buffetings on pillion
of motor bike they pull up.
                    Police car

circles block, while I bend over—

looking for coins I haven't lost
in the gutter,
            searching by feet, kerb-dark
for an unsuspiciousness.

Anxieties

Words like 'ineffective'
                        come to mind,
with fear of something ultimate.

Ineptness. Of course we know life's
not lived t' the full
or empty;
but fear

hampers wordlessness
at verbal approximates, tongues
lag from their speech
to say nothing ultimate. Just
once is enough
for thinking things through
to the end.
          Shout
for echoes, listen—

to metallic sound of stones
                        ring
on some dry creek bed, down from

cwm wall analysis.

Experience
uncomfortable
with words only
at their end

where the cliff rises, boyish
insults, doggerel falls.

The dusk filters through

The dusk filters through—
permeable membranes;

banks up, darkness;
sifts down, mist.

We welcome the lack of clarity
close up. The night is un. This is

unusual for the time to come.

Ageing Acceptances

                Natural
rhythms: going slow now
into middle age—at pace
to accept it. Shifting down after
with impotence? You want

'the inevitable as the natural'? Don't
think of bad/goods or the
reluctance. 'd be just one
or its only closed option. You

come out from ramp up to the stadium,
which is also the ramp down
and you
prance some light steps on cold concrete

to get a look.

Sun-Following

Reveille,
        the night;
revelry,
the ebb
      to day.

Peace on the beaches,
                    homeless
by granules.

A Change Blowing Up

Lit ribs
in night cloud above harbour.
Night winds stir water,
                        move black rucks white
scums in darkness.
              Yet,
they have for yet not reached me. Troughs
in buffetings leavings lip. Flags
                freshen,
                stiff-
                      en—
                  ripple ends.
Low
     luff swells
at above mooring, with a rise pre-change
                                      before
a wind cracks open my sails.

Dispossessed

to Sally

In the
quiet of the night
before
dayfall
I ask you for
remembrance in your sleep,
dreams if you have them. To

enter, us after,
strip
onto
 silk body, go
over moonscape skin
 no
human. Come to—only

after very very light
god-play. We

can sleep now. It'll feel
a long time till we're rising.

 Daybreak—

red, blue balloons,
circulating from the past,
rising still, out lob-lifted
onto Spring air.

The Nurse Carrying My Suitcases

Up and about but
no strength—
            dazzled
in cold May sunlight.

Autumn, oblique
cuts—
        slants
to rays' edge.
Down

through their centre—
                    bright
light,
    full
onto grass's down-
                gradings
from reach of building. Glowings

absorbed, emitted,
through transparent skin,
hung comfortable
around dull storages
of light. The small
                nurse

bustling me out with my
suitcases,
        weak
as walked
        white cement
of a path beside her—

graded to cut
the curved lawns.

             What

left behind, on the path?
                        Not
mine, their pain—
                 the cut-scrape
of a tonsilectomy's not much
you're to understand a death by. *Their*

pain opened talk,
my inmates. Not
learned in that, no part of it. My life
slept in blood still, when death's
too far off to be warmed by: loves
expanding in sun, like oranges—

dark green leaves
on the Mildura trees.

The 'Set' of Form

Factory

drool-dribbles smoke
upwards into rectangular-built
air-
      shafts onto
horizon.

            Free
                    floating
buoy face of thought, over
pointillisms,
            the pattern, style,
the Nomenclature.

Do we set
steel on steel?

    Brick
chimney, soot greased into,
glazed through.
               A million souls
say approximately working there.

And we would want the numbers.

The Chinese Scroll

First thoughts
I've had for a long time—

where someone's had them for me
and I followed unbelieving, un-
burdened in their belief,
going about my business.

                      Thought-touchings
should be different out of doors
in Autumn.
        The cold moves
down, about knee level among
trees.

     Thoughts

rest like birds on the ground,
                         peck
for food at spot near to

verandah, in the eaves

of this twelfth century Japanese
shingle hut.
       Take down

painting on the wall over the
tatami—
      when Chinese

scroll is rolled tight,
to be tied up, slotted away,

on a spool among library
of mountain sketches. Always, sages

sit cross-legged through mist's edge
in a valley among the peaks.

Otiose

          Not so much the phrasing
but the gestures:
                  words are enough
by themselves, one by one, sky writing
in the cirrus—
                huge aah from cloud smudge,
sky hidden momentarily under trailing
slow puffs of smoke.
              Resign
yourself to your lexicon entry
                    look it up.

           Monoplane buzzes
across summer silence tent-stitched with gnat noise,
red hem, dog yelp. I would withdraw
these words if I just knew that you could take them.
But would you miss them, apart from me?

I've no allegiance—*any*.
                You took 'love',
'sex' 's not worth a snigger—
                      snickered off.
(For instance) you took 'children'—No?
                You've head down
in your heavy scuffle splay. I move out most
directions you could blunder into, give no scope
to lurch my way again—if I've kept 'hope'.

Mantis on Chair

Sunset—daylight saving.
Night's hot, lights burn—

long onto morning.

Praying
mantis, acute angle
middle of dark seat, foot-
placements neat,
delicate as a goat, moves
peduncle-green foreclaw, swivels
triangular head—under-
carriage's opening in.
                    Alert's,
square-turned before eyes
flickered to movement. Stalks
jerk-scales up armrest
to chairback hangs out of

even thinner shadow
tangent to back slope,
light from
two hundred watt light globe
on
the cord straight above it.

Night at Fireworks

The talk doesn't mean much,
doesn't mean
anything—except for the tone
the contact.
We're blessed with the contact.

People
far and apart
           at inar-
ticulateness,
wherever the meaning is—
forgetful against outside them. O-

pinions—bright fireworks

flare,
      fall,
            ember, glitter
in traceries char-floated

warm onto earth through
cool air.

      You go back,
tread round
dark caravans;
tamped earth oil-dank
                what-
ever you have has no dis-
solution.
      Night
           drops

noise in the cool breeze,

light light.

ADDENDA FOR THE FIRST TWO VOLUMES

Docks and Harbour

                    Leaving it
forever, where opinions
float over—matchsticks, cigarettes
on the tide, in, at wharf lengths
along water. You shift

off—
        only stroll—to stay
mobile. Hoots of ships and
underblasts of tugs trans-
mitting motion back onto
unsettlement in and off through
lappings No foot out
on wharf, or hulls up
in docks. No time

to contemplate the flux of time
in—buoy out
in harbour chained
to the fathoms. I make clump
on wharf's wood, ring riveted plank
lengths to bolts loose
at the underpinning girders. Air

washes off-shore lighter
than the tide, and flows through,
not wetting wharf, to planks'
juts-out on sea's side.

Working Outside

                    Basic
functions outdoors, sweating
and shitting, pushing hair back
off sweat-brow, blowing fart-ruffles
down trouser leg, bending back
again shovelling dirt out
of a ditch, excavating hole dug
to set stumps for a large shed
foundation. The air comes

up, currents lightness
or denseness, wavering across at cross-
currents, not from the stagnant
waters.

            Stump posts
concreted in, then nailing
floor joists, wood framework, corrugated
iron roof for exposed wood
protection. The weatherboards

nailed on after setting sash
frames—for lead lattices
that will take wind and accompanying
stress fractures over years, crack-
gauges measuring-out lives lived

as a constant.

Fishing Tackle

                I lack commitment
to my students for Instance?
                            You take
some easy way out of this for me—with my students.
The fixities

of intention—lain like nets at midnight,
off-shore,
              next to the lighthouse. What

system in blues blacker than black?

Swells
rise, part-shape themselves at neap tide, to be

cross-stirred from prevailing winds as we

make a haul.

LEAVETAKINGS

Midnight Bell at Chion-in

Motions in emotion:
continuum from detail
to separate out a you that have lived
through. Heard

at Honenji bell so deep
the sound was below human
pitch—yet could make out
vibration under foot, under
tone. Organs

shake floors, this muffled
by earth, but air ripples,
volume-solids buffeting
the head. Heard

whatever there was to hear. End
dangled off boom's
jangle. Boom swung,
once into twice.
Once again Night

had set in much earlier—
Midnight: night's night,
sunk into forgetting
people, their absences. New Year's

Eve: the revelry
had stopped to boom's boom,
the one hundred and eight
tollings. Earth dampers
shake, and damp
up through earth freezing;
but it breaks out in fountain, children

laughing shouting lower down
off the hill.

Some Comforting for Age

        What then would lift us? Sex—
repulsed at dry aged skin,
rucked kapok mattress, the bed made
a long tine ago—
not to be slept in, wanting
comforts of the aged—
they get a little sleep on.

        Why
such guilt when it is simple—
given we are simple. We
are not.
    Believe we are,
          that
it is 'easy',

when we have stepped out of bed,
as out of an affection,

to get some little sleep on by
ourselves,

from fears to be alone, fears
not had till we'd the company in them.
        Still,

what we do with a life is our own—
none too close
to anyone—if we'd talk with them,
sing with them about anything
but that—
    love words—

that walk, that talk, close to the ground.

To Stop My Thinking With

                The reluctance
to do anything—to do anything
wrong … To do
anything.
           We thought

with activity to make out
on our feet. Had been settled
before we had
   ever got on to them.

Preparing and Eating an Evening Meal

Dozing a little death-
                    sleep,
sleep-walking off from own body,
lying down in doze-daze
memory of where awake could be
from here.
           Slipped out back way,
away from any front way, re-
enter through door un-
understanding unundersanding. Purchased

the fish at old fish market—
slither, glisten, gaff hook's
up to butcher's apron. Out market

onto wet streets, the pavement, pushing
newspaper parcel tight
                      between
jumper, plastic coat, to keep off
rain—it and me. Wet

rails along to tram
reflected off iron pipes railing
a safety zone. Wet,
the tram itself, green,
unabsorbent, deflecting flicking off
rain. No home

to go to, just flat,
and cook food pretty messily after'd
gutted, scraped off
scales.
      Warm
inside, listen into

radio. Rain pounds,
lollops heavily.
But can hear swish to car wheels more

than can hear motors. Reflections—
lights—off roads—dulled:
from everywhere. You

can sleep too heavily by the heater
to need
        go back room in the dark.

Stamina for Some Other Purpose

'…if rescuable'—
                    azaleas
potted, plastic tub—
cement-heavy, plastic's
too hard to grip. Moved—
my face averted
                    from almost purple
red flowers.
        Heavy

as bases to a portico never built
on-
to back of the house where stood the two-
yard-wide verandah,

slim corner posts, mouldings
holding onto the shafts,

balustrades at the side:

glassless now roofless.
Wind in rain moving up through spaces
underhung from the eaves
merely.

        Had gone out,
to come back in from not-home,
to find out what home is. Night

draws off from buildings, fences,
colours not hues to them.
                        A Pissarro snow
thoroughfare's distant bluestone building
against a grey sky.

            The rhythms
in snowfall, freeze's drift-practice,
exercises of an animal
in dying, life-stamina
stretched out into tiredness. The
evening retains light
as mementoes of the day;
still damp with them.
                  Eyes

concentrate onto furthers,
into the surrounds. A wall's white
plaster in dark—

floats off from building,
as if off a jetty.
We

hold back
from finality
in dark.

      Get the wood
as well as kindling. Should be plenty,
for I stacked some, over at the triangular pile

where I split the half-logs earlier.

Water Surface Light

The indulgences I allow myself.
A few only at a time.
A lifetime.

          To get myself
straight. To understand
where it stop/starts without me, to
make it clear what
the human is, what
the non-human contrasts with.

                            I leave
anyone—I leave her
particularly—my body,
myself if she wants it.
I never did, except
in negatives, inertias
at custom, links
to an understanding of what I must
endure.
        Life

goes on—
          outside
any recollection of others, the
fragility of their recollection. Sunlight—

full, patch on a wall,
and reflected off bottle surface, onto
iron bedstead, sheets,
spare room of a house
that should be empty of me.
                          Any
love is oblique

out from that hope.
                    It has

not aged. I thought,
felt like that, even when
I did not remember so much
backwards—

            when closed in
to the forms as they have lasted
is memory, not here,
not anywhere, substance
from some other time than yesterday.

From Cars to the Beach and Gulls

           White
edge round car hull, sharp to
cut-curve of duco, still,
on vacancy around.
                Purpose:
efficiency in shock flow,
                    to
wade solid air within
streamlined pressure among
forms.
       Bird

by bitumen preens wing,
beak point swivelling down
feathers onto wingpit, in the
grey reductive hang
to air—
        winter,
a half-light clarity. Felt

eye-touch off surface,
vapours weightless,
wetless,
        easily
lifted.

        White
comes through on sight
too quickly—
          before
we have been
         taught
in the light's relativities,
the conformation among hulks. A

cincture mark
where the belt has been
             holds up
lines of the flesh—
the nothings it weights to. I
move across, step among
Drumstick wrapper, papers, past
cars and onto
the beach—where sand
spreads into vast widths
to ocean. There

the gull walks bandy
as a penguin after circling in, wings
gathering up, from beach
the dips of air.

Failures

                        Worn out
with people who come up to me—
would be better if passing by. Sit,
music as background
for conversation best to be gotten through
quickly,
        efficiently—
unfinally.
          Life

is so *long*, full of repeats;
the unrepeats irritate
but renew me. Is it
conclusion that one would have?
                            Fell

in love but miffed it,
sleeping with a friend
who was *only* a friend.
                      Honour

teaches us whatever
we are, mimes it to us
practising it on our faces, feeling
the intricacies in them. She

shacked up with an analyst,
after period in a psychiatric
ward had played on fears,
white keys. She

went she said close to
shock treatment—as 'therapy'.
I slipped, nearly slithered under

a tram, like motor bike
onto wet steel rails. Twenty

years—not quite,
                          but who
can count back accurately
in time, measure sequences
to the thin lines of a calendar? Has
gone, none returned
(not me either). Pride
kept me off too late
with a pretence I was whole. What

expect? We're finished?
Me too?
          The
stories are gristly. Baby
dropped on cement path. Nights
spent with 'friends'
in the system, after breaking out
from the psychiatric ward
and the hospital and a constriction
that had come through from there, been
'realised'.

              Babies?

Real too?
          Yes,

probably. Life's
melodrama as I've seen it, seen
my friends see it, in whole
failures of our understanding. Sit

open air concert, after
hot curry, conversation,
dim white shirts. Watch

the flare fall of cool
Bengal lights, bright showers
dropping, on a break in sitar music,
in the dark summer heats.

Keeping It Together

                    Wholes
fragmented—cannot
de-segment parts
into wholeness. The Gods—

whatever—drove us, iron spikes
into the earth, pitching

marquees from us, tent stretched,
bunting scrape against flap, to
swell canvas up over

the misshapen iron, spread-flattened,
made malleable off jerked dints

from the alternating mallets.

Faces in Cold

Whatever happens
                just happens—notion
as real as the real, as the
'illusory'. We

could hardly want it otherwise. Slow speech,
little understood, of a woman in labour,
tired of it all except…
              it all. Where

there is birth, death, there is something—
whatever is to be confronted with, in death.
                                Clean words,

for and against each other—to be used
sparingly. Burning off, night's
cold. Bonfire:
white hair, faces on dark
overcoats—memory
as a keepsake in cold. Put

the dried branches on it, it
could do with some more.

Options

                        A kind
of despair at not despairing. I have
no interest in myself
for myself. Kept merely
for repetition, for the meaning
in that. Once

would've wanted to know what me, older,
would be like. Well it's not different
enough, is habit—and

no place I would have wanted
to be—that is to be
forever.
           Make void

in a dropper, drip drips with it
onto infusion in glass,
                             red
tinct where it's droppered.

Loosed from Music

                The clearances
to bring emptiness in—

and make it solid, have
no resonances in it
                   onto
vibration.

        The wind shoves

at door scritch, reopens
upon gust, swung back
into slack,
           Wood

of structure joined to something
specific, fitted, hinged

onto space they've wade for it.,

Frost Breath

                        In frost,
out. The Southern Cross half-
buried in a rust-coloured
night roof. The Pointers
waver-twinkling down
onto it.
        Steam-breath
expanding across frost line
onto sharp air.

               You
do not take easily
to intruders. No possessions,
no need. Anything
will contain everything that is not
you. No people,
no idea of them. The world moves
close up, surfaces
as depths—
           lost

in the 'were' time, the once without
opening.

Thinking Unsuccess

What I do now?—worthless. What I fail to do,
worthless—but the hangover!
                      It takes

nothing to do nothing un-
successfully.

                    Thinking as an

activity—
           woman leaves me
forever—

I think about it
forever.
       Inactivity's
my comment, getting straight
the completed work in inaction. Forms

my moral community—
                          reflex
pre-instinctive, outwards
from a forever not needing to be done,

to an afterwards, when it will never be done.

Solo Concert

Pop songs
traced out
on guitar, light filament.
They were singing songs like that in Cromwell's
army—*Greensleeves*.
Meaning, in present,
from past known as past, string
oscillating down soundbox
onto memory. Blind

guitarist picks way
on vibration, slips fingers
across fretboard—there is nowhere
to go that has not been
gone.
      Empty

seats up between full. Floor,
cellophane wrappers from packets, to
harmonise into resonant
gaps. Applause. Audience

empties out auditorium
through collapsible wooden seats, bent
back from their bench rows

through the hall.

Worth Living

               Flies
settled onto area
dog'd scratched free
to ease itch off the settling. Im-
patience more mine
than the dog's. After half-

summer it was blood clot
scratched parti-fresh—flies
clustered on like a blood clot
above it. We tied cloth

round nose, put pads
on his paws to keep from scratching, used
liniment and a repellant
against flies. It tore pads

with teeth, was crazed
by the repellant, even liniment—
but grateful for any treatment,
and hangdog among quilts
of flies. I never saw

such life, nor
would've seen it again.

The Presences

                      Iron
swivelled along down trouser leg
onto cuff. Pressed separately. Steam,
finished—iron settled back
onto butt. We will watch the tele-
vision, sit to see it
together,
          into the long night's
sleep.

     The balances—
the presences—
             with you
in you—in-

termittent.
         Commercial break.
Make tea,
        dip tea bag
in stained water. The realis-

ation of an image
off the old black-and-white with
colour set—fills blue
flicker over the walls
with quantum of the light
of day. Get up.

Switch off heater.
The cold just perceptible.
Shock at passage, through
onto bedroom, ice air.

Oblation before Entering the Temple

                    Re-
plenish stone basin—
bamboo spout
at lipped edge—to

issue onto hands,
                rinsed
mouth as an admonition
to silence,
        washed under

bamboo. Speak quietly,
the purity in water.

Broken Foot

Just try it one
more time—the coming here,
return back to your homeland—
as if that ever did mean
'home'.
          Have learnt to walk
like baby, placing foot
at crutch and swing off shoulders,
to glide jerk at next step. Over
room, couch armrests
as launching pads. The sticks creak
onto weight on small points; foot
feels floor like hand, to balance
an acrobat hand-standing. You switch
off hi-fi set, switch sticks, sway weight
onto back door.

          To change
clutch with heel. On bitumen,
white lines down banks of lawn. To watch
road for part-clearances
among schoolchildren.

With You

Wherever I went
you went—
me tagging along
in front of you
'for your sake'
and ours. A German

cathedral, walled into walled
street—spire receding up
medieval air through
perspective, clouds separating
across vapours. Dip fingers

into stoup of holy water and rejoin
traffic. Your visit

was into damp stone, mine
was in the 'Middle Ages' where
you tried to join me. Still
feeling its age—it might have been any
age. I see it as

the Past, as 'history':
I feel it 'through time',
through hundreds of years whatever that might
mean. The crowds speak

French not German.
A side road runs cobbled down
narrow streets bent back—stones
clinked under steel plates, time
ricochetting off a wall. The traffic

down alley street not recent
but contemporary. A carillon of medieval
bells jangles out through
and up.

Recollections

              My
schooldays are gone,
so too are my love days,
when was some *openness*
to live in.
          Wanting

something to stop
my thinking with, thinking
through what I am now,
will become.

Gathering and Dispersal

                        Tipped up
earthworms from underside
of a doormat, making humus
from fibre. Cleared
weeds out of gutter next
t' fence, so drainwater
could trickle back through drain to main
flow.
      Trees

drop their leaves
                one by one
but frequently—
                onto roof—
earth mulch in spout, smoulder-
erosion to the work programs
of time.
      Still dry

where I shifted car in the rain.
Come summer it won't give shade
as lasting as a dry spot
from this rain shelter. I drive

off, foot to clutch pedal
and accelerator. Over the town, rain
gyrates out of wind helixes—
and comes down.

Leavetaking

                    Liner
moving sideways off dock
out of lee water. Friends stopping
on deck, numberable at iron
post. Tossed streamers

cross down onto curved sides
of liner, disconnected off
by tugs. Her mouth puffs

Hello, drops syllable.
                    Ad-

vice scatters—names, laughs—
flowers in rosettes, fades

across water onto silence, rides
surface, takes weight
onto dark. My feet se-

cure from slip under
iron lattice under guard rail. I

leave, move off against
press against rail, turn
back on heel, walk ringing wharf's
iron deck on way out.

ADDENDUM TO
LEAVETAKINGS

Along a Nature Strip

>   (1)

>   And meat eaters
turn me off—dog's cloying
shit, hind legs yanking
dry grass from a lamp post. Easing
off squat, not
>   ready to bark,
standing erect, defending its ground
yet. A dog's life
is your life.

>   (2)

>   I weight foot,
down into dogshit
like gums, learn to put foot
onto, on concrete
together. Draw in from
breath off the wet
horizons.

>   (3)

>   This is not much
of an era—
>   though Before's

still there: brick chimneys, clay

pots, fan leadlight—red
rose seccateured
on its stem—lead framing
black along at the human

measurements.
                Some thought
we could do this all, together still,
once again.

SLEEPING IT OFF

Sleeping It Off

Unbound the shanghai
to lug stone in bed out off the
verandah onto the mating
cats. Their yodelling

seasonals other nights kept me
awake long after I'd bedded down. By
midnight now finally I'd
dispersed them. Not sure

from the bump skid shriek on
to scatter if I'd hit one
or not. And lost

sleep: have lost whole lifetimes
of sleep—be unrecovered
if extended into further lifetimes
by a me still kept wake enough
to be aware of them. The cats

themselves would've been dead
most of these tines of sleeping/waking,
hit by skim of stone much sharper-
edged off thong-thwack
of rubber, crippled—given a shot—
by rheumatism, so ready for
the vet's needle, though not his time
of appointment (sharp-clawed,
and quick enough yet to be unholdable
down). I've lasted long times

myself since seeing grey fur
mobile under street globe, looped
fence, gap separating it
from a hedge. Don't go

back to see it, still sees
me, close up boy: not
moved off, moved on,
and our bodies are the same.

Mnemonics

                All talk
relegated to whatever meanings
are to come. Corridors

passageways down nineteenth century
houses, unrenovated as
divided into flats for cheap
rent. Under a twelve foot

ceiling, at the jambs,
your voice draught to lintel holding
plaster cracked under heavy shut
doors. Wasn't going
to seek, couldn't find.
"More air than talk."

                      Others've been

demolished, renovated, wallpaper
embossed, pasted over
walls in long passageways gold-
lit. Lumps of plaster crushed to
powder by the hobnail
boots. No photograph

of unpolished floor, dark stain before
the sander—shifted furniture—or
of walls of passageway before we'd stripped
bricks—surface rough now, but
more level than the plaster—no

record of difference—undated but still new.

The forms make space
from the walls they were set to.

Doppelgängers

      Come back into

the aquarium, where fish
form doppelgängers at tank corners,
parallel diagonals from
the sides off sealed edge, dorsal

fins flicker cut curves around
labyrinth not walled into

the glass, parallel too
gliding at the straight
in its place, flick-deviates

and each fish is the original.

Possessive Adjectives

                      Return
to me, back from *my* dead? Say
anything that you recollect
from back there. You/me

listening to talk, speculating
on whatever. A removal truck

backed up at the door, furniture,
chairs stacked on, inside—you
knew what it was. It was

your past, not mine, 'ours'
—tailgate fastened—memories
forgotten—as how it removed ourselves
from its ends.

Shifting Fortifications

for Dianne

           Late night
ribaldry, work shoes off
from untied knots, strip shirt
up off away chest sweats in
beads. Bodies free of a cloth-

touch, cooling under the self-
sweat. White sheets and hot
other jostling space
above them under wettings
of laughter. Dig moats

and sand castles with toy spades. Dip-drag
buckets from the edge of
the ocean. Bury normality, packed
in wet, up to laughing heads
in the sand.

Insecticide

The geography of the body—nerves
rivers, the floodflow
where they went. We had

this problem about ants—
lines twitching, ants nosing,
scabs of ants on coca cola
spillings, opened tins of canned
meat. Wash,

wipe them all off. Un-

killable crushed only
with the fingers. More efficiently
(advice given specifically
for cockroaches): "Use cruelty,
they'll find somewhere else. I
burn them".
                Hot water's

needed anyhow—getting off
grease. Use hot;
then after, cold water. The

body's sensitive
(to ants as to its own
needs—as I am: then
I *live* with it).
                Carry can

of insecticide down garden path
through air to anthole, and go down
on my knees, drip solution in

from
        the nozzle onto the hole.

The R.S.L. Reunion

                Who
finished it then? Our fathers? They took
backwards to the times. Not
their own way, had it shown them;

but 'took it to their advantage'.
                          Felt

hat with the sweatband
and feathers on. Square
slouch to jaw, easing
the gum, before caries
would have their teeth out. In-
comprehension of the missus —
a silent hatred, 'tac-
iturn'. Who'd

care for their opinions
now? The flags
on the flagpoles at the R.S.L.
hall
      stay floodlit
in white arches of the portico, each
month monday—
                  that'd be
tonight.

Keg

beer before, after,
in especially, the reunions,
insulates them at a sense
of that war when they were young,
rough, humorous—tac-

iturn.
        As usual —

over by ten o'clock.
The parked Holdens move out, un-
troubled about their indicators,
into unfilled traffic lanes off next
to the kerb.

In Concern

Violence with knives, knives
for peeling apples, breadknife's
shaft in wood, plastic handle
rivetted in through back onto spot
brass. Any edge

will make cuts if mishandled. I
slice fruit, make cuts to core
and slip. Inability's
feebleness at judging in-
abilities. Shaft's

one aim—is not to be cutting
bread.
        Interest

fresh in from its time off—
not my time. Resonance

sharpening up for the new
once. I get up,

walk to door, open own
echoes in the passage, conclusion

arriving in under-lethargies
from the dead.

Recognitions

(for Ian, after)

Twenty years
              on—it might as well
be the end of a century, as well
our children as us, grown old,
ageing with us. You make quite

a size of it, measuring out
space between us, synchronising
time to the activity, bulk in
waste.
      I suppose though

our body shrinks, I suppose it *has*
shrunk, gathering in
to the nought that it has come from, filling
at stop. Moment in,

not of, apprehended
quantified as a whole. Shout
to whisper through to the silences
among friends.

Jay-Walking

            Used
bootbrush with polish, tan
smeared onto uppers, leather
stitched into tuck at sole's
edge. Shine-wipe
with cloth. Smart,

easing legs, body, out
of car: woman cocks

up knees in seat tilt, shone
boots reflect thighs down
from leather.   Frees the legs,
dusts the skirt down, pivots
heels to spike holes in soft
asphalt, jolts tra-
verse of road over
camber, crosses then at
concrete kerb onto
other side. Mingles

at pace variation among
people in traffic flow, snag-
currents cross-eddying
through our stares.

Top Forty or Whatever They're Called Now

Chlorine in my throat, itch
at the back of the lungs, steam off the heated
pool.
      Outside

against air douche, steadying spine, back
on the leg tendinitis—listening
in effort to say something to you,
who have ceased trying to say it. Nothing

to do, nothing to say;
I certainly wouldn't want you to hear me
whistle it.
      Guitar wire—

through half-open car window
within panels over wheels, concrete—

oscillating outside comfort.

The Japanese Buddhist Cemetery

Stone path through graveyard
among memorials the shape
of Greek urns, glass vases, white
flowers on top
of support stone. Higher, cairn
mementoes, solid geometry
in shape of the Buddhist elements, plaques
graven with names
up above. You cannot ever

imagine yourself
being buried there—you are not
Japanese (neither now,
are they?). Stone slabs

squared into ashlared path's
border, steps drop to the
oratory next the stall by
the hill. Sale of incense being

burnt, embedded in the
incense burner's sand. Don't
buy sticks but do clap
my hands. Turn down hill to

white gravel onto street railed
for streetcars: smudged tree lines, green

cars cross in fine rain, fog
sleet.

After Shutting the Gates

Feeding times at the zoo,
                     sides of meat, blood
dragged on ground to cages,
pails slop offal. Cat
cuffs mate,
            to scuff-haul at meat hunks,
before lying on bellies,
               nuzzle-muzzlings, teeth
and tongue picking out strands among
                       the tendons. Attendant

bolts gate, lugs carcass off truck,
hangs slippery liver from a free
hand, closes to gate on black leopard pacing
the double mesh, tosses liver in, secures
gate on outer wire, opens inner
from angle to slip meat through; shuts locks
                       bolts each
gate to respective fence. Leopard twists
spine,
      getting jaw on purchase,
                       stretches neck
vertebrae.   At all other zoos

they just chuck the meat over.
                   Hunting
is not in single-valued logic.
               The life-quarry's

silence at evening sends
        chill to the neighbouring suburbs
in wave roars some distance off. The calls
are as un-

        recognisable as the jungle,
          off the reserves. Lynxes, tigers,
big cat hunters,

in silence at last,

lie prone on ground like branches.

Carrying On

                    Lean
head under hood, black dress working
the farm after death of her husband,
the children gone. Milked
cows in a half-dark before sunrise, white
with black patches bulging
out of shadows using
both milking machines and the pails. Had invited

me in off the highway through passage
for tea, milk jug, stainless steel sugar bowls,
the cups and saucers left over from different
sets. No idea

what she had made of me: youth
first, and was not a local, that she could
talk outside their gossip—who'd take
no notice of me anyhow. (Butter
split, whacked from wooden pats, flicked
off onto greased paper, scales;
sugar scooped from sack.) I
insisted tactlessly on paying, and
was very young.
              Had she any

idea of my thoughts on her? A legend,
certainly, maintaining the farm
still, the family gone, life
gone on after, pigs and cows
no human, footsteps related
to their own sound, chair drawn up
at the periphery between sound and silence.
                          It stays

open, the past, now.
And I know it, unknow it—and can't unlearn it
back in. If closed off,
would be as our beginnings themselves closed off
at the other end in birth, parents—
through whatever gap in childhood—dark
mother now bent, old woman, myself
middle aged man her son, not knowing her
all too well—our age between us—
as remote in ends from each other as span

out of time of the Ptolemies.

The Tarot Reading

                  She laid out
cards between butting cig-
arettes, not inhaling
till she'd curved deck back under
her thumb, did drawback, stubbed,
ground butt while meditating
on smoke lifting. Client followed

first card, vetted in-
terpretation, the next: corres-
pondence in arcana
and suits, getting sequences
together. Barge, flat-bottomed,

hauling shale quarried
from deposits, water slipping along
bows, knocking rocking its own
wash. Client grateful, con-

fused, grateful to be
confused, canals out into
unmapped suburbs, canal locks to
confusion. Bead

curtains mingle rustle
with pelmets, flap body
of sandlewood incense from
carpet, ash tubular across
brass. Drops onto
grate, breaks; smoke hangs—
droops, spread-lifts. Her
clothes shift worn cloth across
bulk. We discuss

customers as patients through
to kitchen. Coffee boiled thick. Fortune
makes room from smoke ajar in
wind's return.

Unalienated

                Mars
within twig branches stencilled
upon blue, orange hanging
on dark. Night sealed in at
horizon onto the raw,
fresh.

      A lover and
a friend, fingers doubled at
knuckle joints. Walked together past
picket fence next door, fence
in iron stakes—back of hands and
finger nails flicking the fleur de lis
ends.
         News was

of Hungarian, mum's lover, making
phone calls twitching guilt to sex-
violence. "What's my name? Am
Death."
         The stars

are a long way off. Sympathy's
lost out through the distances
in there. No sense of
a me that is locatable among
the stars. I saw the night

out, day in, when
young   to prove the neon
darkness would terminate
in the eternal.
            Dawn
is colder than night.

The warmth is already visible
                              but not
there. Our lives

are as small and as distant as
the stars—even, under them,
our deaths are. From ever-
lasting to everlasting, no
spaces left in a universe
for us.
       Cold storage

in caves below the day.
                       Stars
at freezing point. Frost lays
white
under
         side-shifts to a full
moon.

Loading Beer Barrels

                Force
applied getting wood firkin
up ramp;
        wedged, foot;
grip iron hoops at sway-rolling
off side; hoist lift-levering—
bump-falls onto rail truck,
t' be shunted off 'nd be coupled. Sweat,
anxiety at hitch, effort, getting

it on. Trucks, unlinked—
buffered off from an engine
to recoil along rails, bump
onto mobs of themselves, direct forward
straggle. Rails criss-cross, curve
back onto restraightening
to recurve; join, separate, cross
across angles into recurving
to restraighten. You prop forward,

strut the next barrel
off decline's roll-back. No trucks
from these shuntings-up
                    to complete storage
on.

The Length of the Spell — Three Episodes

        (I)

Barge boards warp across
weft outwards.
        Paint

dry at flaked off underneath
of the house. No sun,

except in flash; we in-
fer from its weight, which c'n
squat under.

        Lift yourself
up to be going
out. There is no
necessity for staying here
at all.

        (II)

        You roll
sleeve up, dip hand
into bucket of well water—slopped
lipped taking water
in well air. Any
solitude is away from you—
has been inferred.

        (III)

    Accustomed
to the length of the spell, we carry

water (ordinarily
from the tap); and boil this
billy.
      Granted,

it's likely to be potable. Drink
deep by yourself. There is no
necessity for staying here
at all.

The Habits

                  Moss
growing up the wall, rain—
wall damp as a consequence. We
sat the verandah boards till it
stopped. Rain sounds
from guttering, spouts as a signal
for sleep. Whose idea was it

to sleep?
         The body says
sleep, keeps closed mind
in possession. No idea
where I can finish this, look back
onto time it had never started.

After the Equinox

                  The bells full
of rain through the air above
the cathedral. Lack of
solidity in time past and
of now. I walk the sparse

grass to mud boundary by
the playing fields onto whatever times
there are, into the temporariness
of the past, slither, no
foothold. And call the days

back—onto moment
from forwards—and watch the dark
set, noonday on, no
wind, lit mist hangs
in twilight—fog bodies
wet ground. Clearing. Hum

of stars rung on far
off from earshot. I watch the night

crystallise out of resonance
in bells.

The Salivation

                Dogs
ageing on, in stages
of life effortlessly, no
apprehension they're growing
old. Had a watchdog

through childhood barked ferociously
at visitors to the side gate, when
opened, clambered licking them,
front paws. It aged

suddenly, dog's pace, winter
hibernated in sunshine, warm
path; summer shifted over
in shadow, fitting its shiftings
on lawn. Reluctant'd amble
adjacent to my space, tolerating
a pat. Found him dead,

bringing meal of butcher's bones
with meat on, down path,
to flick-scrape onto tin plate
in kennel. Body seemed
asleep, neck relaxed
forward into paws. We

buried the dead-limp
body next to dahlias by
the plum tree. Nose pricked
by mint, patch overgrowing fence
like a weed. I forgot

mostly that the body had been
buried there, was cautious

only if ground muddy
round the rotary hanging clothes onto
its wires. Twenty years

on, I've seen the house itself
off and on, scraped mud off
from the garden, scuffed soles further
on mat to clean feet. Climbed
the Jarrah wood of the back stairs
to verandah, snipped fly wire shut, turned
the key in metal lock of the door,

and've gone in.

The Revenant

I went down
to the beach
in winter. Made phone calls
from a booth twisting dial holes
on a jerk—marriage/divorces needing
legal contract, signed now,
with the settlement. Cars passing
attract eyes like animal
movement—too sealed in
for animals: people strapped in
indistinguishable from headrests
upright to safety belts
on their seats. But people

are all around here, crouch down finding
hideouts in the wind or at
shelter sheds from its access off
the harbour. Cars don't

cruise in it—chassis
too heavy, move rudderless through
vacuum pockets, at radials against
a curve. Ocean troughs

swell themselves up out
further onto crests, sharpen
where swollen, foams chopped off
at flurries. Whistlings
along telegraph wires, hummings rolled
tumbling out of reach. Over

cut lawns to amusement
park. Opening time
of Dodgem cars under poles, sparks

at electric net. Bump themselves
through openings, squeezed out
from in traffic, jam-shocked
onto buffers. Attendant slews
apart to clear. Pursuit rumbled
and ram-jarred into flinch-laughs, swivelling
back-jerked against arms askew
on their seats.

Park Near Evening

                Brown
oak leaves, footprints
across lawn, rain glaze
on dry brittle. Leaf mulch

to rock border, raked off from
grass near a hoe-cut
edge. I walk, pick
up tennis ball landed
on gravel; toss it back

where it came from, street cricket, tip
ball and you run. Struck
again, furrows dint, grass
relifts from inertia. Fielder-
bowler reads drift, veers
to direction of flight, foot
thud-breaking, crook'd arm
at returning. Green gathers

about the boy's weightlessness,
and the sound of another boy's voice
sports-commentating. Footsteps
swing with the throw. Counter-

claims: not-out,
in: sounds plop
on silence: Hello. Air's

cold: horizon rays
from dazzle-distance off, in-
fer from its chill it's
a long way. Under

the jumper thud blood, pulse
at neck, perspiration. You

turn on heel to settling in
night: 'Come home'. Background

greys freshen green up
through the quiet.

On Acceptance

        Have been a
dutiful son for forty three
years—no, less—calculate
adolescence and manhood's time
out of it. Unrequested, wear
grey hair and sonhood like
age growing out of me that I
need
        come to acceptance
of. My mother

herself is not doddery
but sharp, hoisting focus
at challenge, cocked head to her
neck damage, but my own role's

of the past, unrecoverable
from the verve even hatred
that put so much energy
in it. I've lived the whole

lifetime as son, met
near-deaths, all the inputs

need monitoring, fewer energies
to me now. Her end finally

will come, heal something
in me, unearth no doubt
other things. I go whistling

up a dark lane in childhood onto
road with parked cars, curved
bodies wheeled off into
gutters along the street.

Immaturations

No parents but a child still, no friends,
but traces of what would've been friendship, given friends.
Or people—only relics.
                       Bulb valves
cone on back of the television screen, in filaments.
Press knob next to it off—after-image
blinkered out on eyes, in recession
on travel down tunnel vision. The love for them

gone, coming back, gone. Time's
moving off, on. Loves'll
stretch if they don't break. Hungers
durable as food.
                    At walk to Luna

Park, buy fairy floss, sugar crystals
in fluff mouthfuls. Later need
more nourishment to warm body/gut,
                                    but the substitute is
what you need, material, non-substantial
and dense.

        Home, open can
of meat; tap out end—the cylindrical
lump ejects as solid as dogfood,
                            pressure marks
on the rim. The life

solid too, the death. Oven mitts

from press of thumbs t' lift hot plate from the oven
onto table before you've burnt yourself
when it's warmed the food
up.

Visiting Hours

Ticket collector's gate, ticket
clipped—hole punched through
on name under. Ticket with
its hole and passenger taking
a journey. Trains

are slower/faster but don't move
sideways. At the end
of the line, where you yourself'll
get off, engines reverse, ram
carriages in on shunt backwards
to buffers, and you

detrain from the halt-jolting
among carriages, put foot down
on metal step plate to
get out.
        Past gate,

ticket collector, exit that's
entrance—others coming in
at handrail through from other side
of the gate. Out onto

pavement darkening wet with light
rain—nearly slipped over
from slidings and retardals
off grating over culvert in to
stormwater drain under-
neath. Wrapping soggy
from Christmas parcel—roller-torn
to tumble across, wet-shredding through on
grate to silt down into
flood estuary. We're on the move

too, as is, sliding
into, off marriages, home deliveries,
different homes t'
be taken away from. Slip out
from ourselves as we understand
them—to uncertain
sense of continuity
as someone. As we wake up
to lie there in the after-effects
of what we've not gone through, into
unrelease. Hospital, ward

for visit. Patients, shonky, jerk-walk,
puffy like the memories
of the dead dead. Loves
known till become unknown, pre-
served as proof that, whoever, they're
not us—unless presence
of the alien is what we are,
among us. Steel cups,
steel trays without instruments. No friends
left—who at reception desk
are to come to or t' be gone to. Still
indifferent if we've companions there
or no one.

The Journey

                Electric
lights pale into clouded dawn,
but dawn nonetheless. Train

at platform, taking in water,
steam off piston valves. Boarded;
door shut to compartment. No

future? You never had
a future—that was finished
before it'd begun.
                  Slept

at night till state border;
wake at railway junction. Difficult
to see round sealed convexity
of the glass. Stopover:

feet, legs stiff
upon platform.
              Breakfast
at a refreshment counter, steams
off coffee, breath.
             Press
of people in wool overcoats, not
everyman but everyone. It's

good to be travelling now.

Work at the Sawmill and After

Backed logs in
through shed
from area adjacent to where they'd been
felled, trunks shoved off
from open end of gable onto
saw to be split up

along lengths into half-moon
cross-sections, dense down onto
depths of logs from cutting edge,
in sounds of tin and wood vibrating
corrugated iron roof's rust
on rafter. Workmen—

'sub-contractors'?—dark singlets,
felt hats, brims dinged down
on S bends, crowns knuckled-in
to split open at corners
of the dinge, bodies thick, im-
mune to pain we would see it
as crabs, arms trunks sur-
prised if nicked not flesh feeling
an agony. Their grubbiness

is our 'structure or design'
though. I turn

on sunset that would go
unrecorded if we'd had ourselves
no use for it— black storm
but horizon opening turquoise
to a slash. As un-
affected by a record
as I would be later, setting

paper alight from a match, puffing
flame up on handbellows used
so bark and kindling near it could
catch fire.
         I head west

to dusk at hill wood's
under-ridge, inadvertently
circling the town and missing the local
pub. Backtracked
in mulch of autumn leaves, crispness
through damp. The town
has not got much but has got it
now. Cold smorgasbord—add
salad, tinned bean mix, buttered
roll on a plate to go with grilled
fish. Some money for it. Black
coffee sweet in glass of cherry
brandy—at television screen's
reflector blurring images off
to the corners on side view. Turn
to thump cannon thud on clicks
as the locals play pool.
         Climb.

up wood staircase. Untuck stiff
sheets. Work the creaking old
bed springs. Join closing time

in the house sounds under sleep.

ADDENDA TO
SLEEPING IT OFF

The Bogongs

        We'd bushwalked up
to a cattleman's hut on the Bogong High
Plain—-checking the maps
and compass, getting lost, turning
back at a river too swollen with thaw
to cross—made attempt, linking
hands to wade/ford it, being near-
dragged off by the current. Climbed

back on Bogong massif by other
route, mounting through hollows and cwms, to
shoulder, out along edge of the high
ridge, peaks. Clouds drifted

in opposite—peaks poking
through—to detach off
from flanks: strata keeping levels
intact, brushed through and around
cliffs. Day grew

hot in thin air, cooling
down as under precipice
at night.
        We'd lit a fire
at fireplace, half-logs balancing gainst
each other, suction drawing air
through vents from within the middle of
the stack.
        Joined

later by some cattlemen as
the fire took, squatting around
among us, sharing instant coffee,
banter, friendly, not all that

interested in what we were, why
wasting time there. Almost,
$$\text{for us,}$$

them being there were the yarns we might have
told about them, them about
themselves—hats dinged down
on heads, brims dipping unsym-
metrically from a curve, hoisting
backside onto bunks, hunched,
faces to the fire, elbows
propped up shoulders leveraged
from the knees, fire subsiding but
flickering on subsidence, char
fiery, logs soggy within
srroulder, rivulets, gulches; talk as
desultory as such flicker into
the night.

Muscle Tone

    Grim grin,
    grimace—
the muscle tone at the lip corners.

    Autonomic
as a response to it
      mine.
           I'm not hankering
           for this subtlety.

           Does it want harsh solutions—
her, me?
      Our purpose'd be
redundant.

Customary Relationship

Dawdling around
hanging about
with death. I've known him quite a long

time—
       who bore each other:
old friends, casual con-
versations picked up in the middle, not just

at gripes—
            hearing each other out

in silence.

From 'Individual Needs'

(1)   You
think I want this again? I don't
want anything: don't even want
to want. Have your
intentions for me, don't ask
that any remain mine.

(2)
And what I want is not to want, too
dead to want is what I want. You'd
give it to me? I don't want
that—from you. Want
Nothing—left ultimately
to itself.

(3)   Disparity
between wants and ends? What happens
fulfils itself, and we wear with it,
and are worn with the completion as
we pass by.

Into Night

                Rainwater
down in culvert under a steep
slope—volumes
dropping, wetting stones under
trees. A redbrick private

school, sandstone quoins along
walls to the chapel, sports
oval levelled, bulldozer by a
cliff. Normally,

benches sit spectators by
a concrete cricket pitch. Now
night—chill winds off
the Derwent. Pylons

to suspension bridge from shore, gold
cables looping down to down, as
highway's narrowed, two lanes from
the gorge. Lights up
through mountain mist and shadow, slip in,
out at different depths, twilight
back of me but deepening beyond
lit neon. Float

heights like a ghost, forget
breath and the distance. Close
underfoot ground darker than
linked spaces on the bridge.

Moving Off

Morning hut,
            crunching around in snow.
Sunrise warmth on woollen gloves—up
touches one's face across valleys. The shadow of
the mountain hut crosses the snow side-on

like blade edge of a knife.

Cha-no-yu

        Squat back
on heels, insteps compressed
to the floor; bend body over
across knees, touching forehead onto
tatami mat; push weight up
with hands' heels from brown stitched
cloth borders lining rectangular framed
gap for fit-shiftings
in straw.

        Mud walls end—
stained quads mortised to stained
uprights: the roofline,
the floorline; wood panelling,
earth walls. Bend over commencing

cha-no-yu: swivelling
body off central spine, the

whiskings, pourings, stoppings
to pause. Four-and-a-half-mat hut

room is cleared space
                        into
rectangular from a square. Be emptied

or filled without contraction,

expansion.

An Open Air Fight

        We'd checked
canal bank, looking along
either side for a site to start
a fight on, getting both
an engagement and the disengagement
over. Yesterday,
we put it off—-he'd swum at the baths
then. A couple of hundred "students",

all grades, crowded paths by
the canal and up top across
road, leaving slopes between—
with rusted car chassis, rabbit warrens—to
make site for an opening
of hostilities. We kept losing

balance throwing roundarms
in the general direction
of an opponent, doing much more
clinch/stand up wrestling
than punching, clutching holds
                        in
close just to stop top-
pling over.
          The non-paying

customers thought they'd some right
to be critical, even hypercritical
of the performance, and an overcrowdedness
of venue they themselves had
set up, made complaints—un-
believable this!—at the lack of a clear
result (had they lain
bets on?). We two

were the only ones with the decency
t' give excuses, blaming correctly
the terrain, slope and selfishness
of the spectators. Should've
donned white coats, sold peanuts—
from bags off trays—making
a mint out of the non-events
there. He managed,

as far as I know, getting swim in
at the baths, one of the only two
days of the week
they'd been open. I look back
on me then, lurching haymakers
in air, asking what
the hell's the connection
to me now? whoever that
might be, and presuming
I'd remember it. Wasn't very
good at brawling, ninth, tenth
in the class—or just a notch
higher; but neither, then,
was he. And it's a good tale

to tell, getting laughs
over our inability to throw a straight
left. Yet the events had

end of a sort, in a time remains
its own not ours, finally
unverifiable as our memories of it
or of the gaps in those years.

Games' Venues

Some skid, some rolled pennies
on lino, sank in genuflexion
to slide them in, came up counter
at attitude for Enquiry, bent
adjudicating by inspection which was
closest, fingernailing up
from edges off the floor to toss
again, ensuring only
that public corridor from the lift was still
empty.

    Lost a few bob

at that. One could make pennies
cushion off on the boards and scoop
the pool.
        It never left us
broke.

    Building's

gone that we skid coins
along. Wrecker's balls knocked out
bricks; sand mortar crumbled
from bricks and concrete; subsequently
bulldozers excavating down
to foundations at full quarrying
depths. Though stop-starts the same

bumper-to-bumper traffic along
Swanston Street. You'd be going to fit
cars in at chrome juxtapositions
down there. Most of the officers too

dead or retired. We were just passing
through—in our working hours—sliding
coins along floor of a building that'd be
air now
         in the lane sites where more

excavation's begun.

On the Money

               Bookies taking

bets in cash, laying off some
of the money held, switching odds, twisting
wooden pegs down line on wood
boards. Clerk's stuffed/withdrawing
notes from Gladstone bag, tots up
numbers in his notebook, snaps
leathers together in iron locking
piece. I pace around

like horses in the enclosure, almost
trotting before debouching single
file—one or two stragglers catching
up—out by gate through onto
track. Orange silks, crimson,
mauve panels rolling off at
the hips.
               Races?

A spectacle in themselves but how
can you wager odds on a cavalry charge
like that?! strolling through
from bookie onto bookie even
after you've lain bets. Checking
the odds? Hardly. Thoroughbreds out

on track had at least jobs
to do. I *needed* t' have
a job to do. Winning left

me high and dry, still in gambling
mode—coitus
interruptus?
              Days

when you've lost…? Abstracted
but relieved!
              Cleaning up after

near rails' bookmakers—price boards
left out overnight—
with odds still up
for close of the last
                      race. Used betting slips

speared down onto spikes. Bookies,
clerks starting motors, heaving their
bags off into opened up

boots of cars.

The Church Dance

We'd wait around
                outside
the hall, after the bush
dance,
        tamping earth smooth over
clearing above mud levels
and bumps, jigging the feet, hands
in pockets waiting for girls to take one
home along a creek bed or
by path up on
                top of its high
banks; climb off track by paddock
fence to front gate, search
for latch under a hedge within
moon shadow,
                then creak in,
bent down under a window past
Checkpoint Charlie: "Is that you,
Ethel?"—from her bedroom
in sleep. Or stop out close to
gatepost mixing "life"
(spoken), sex (unspoken
but done—or almost done) to
separate off to unsettlements
of the future.
                Future's still

unsettled—that's for both of us
apart—twanged strings un-
strung from life, left over
where we'd discarded them, loose wires
to mend a fence with, make do, bight
fastened around top of a fence
post, with the wire ends

re-twisted. Should, later then,
have uprooted the same fence posts, dug
them out, post-hole diggers, tamped
earth back in after as
our feet had once, bumping next
to front of the feet
                      of the pneumatic
tampers. There were nights too

I'd
    just stroll out among
the stars, window-shopping—God
knows what the price'd be! Check
the nomenclature: Aldebaran
over there; Southern Cross—
Pointers of course; Big Dipper;
which one would be the most
intense, what's its precise
candlepower—the amount of light
that could make it through to here *would* be
much the same as a candle's at
this distance. The tracks home
through moonlight were as negotiable
as by day—looking unfamiliar
however as eyes adjusted
to moon shadow. Landmarks:

silver gum at clearing, bend
at fork, a road crossed
in moonlight, the farmhouse
above excavated slopes, glints
in grades of quartz. Quite alone

felt much the same as in company. The invisible
night was maternal,
and kind but not our world. It was
the future before us,
                    kept its distances from us
before.

Reworkings, Inactivities

    (1)

       Took a load
to the tip on the trailer
before closing time. Rain laying
dust kicked up—-litter
over site. Bulldozer
revolves rubbish rolled off
on smoulder.
         Take turns backing
loads in by rear end to
tip head. Dust sifted through

vehicle, hair, clothes. New layers
of whatever's been just unloaded, still a-
waiting the full accumulations, still
                untowed
off to being burnt.

    (2)

        Ruche:
needle at corrugations along a
hem. Thread tugged out
tight into height at
shoulder. Retracted

stitch to retightening
of thread. Holes re-
entered through withdrawals
of needle.

(3)

Lay gasping on
bank after, to vomit up
water—lungs' ballast under
oil slick to suck in
pure air.
        I roll off

wet socks, wring them out.
A wind dries, faint warmth.
Winter sun cloud
              pallor as
a moon. I catch

reflexes shivering up trunk
from feet legs onto neck spasm, ease

jaw cramp, work calf muscles, flex
the feet.

Anaesthetic

Lying reeling
out of chloroform: water pressure through
nasal cavities at a douche-sluice
through sinuses, mucus dis-
                        lodged,
nostrils into a kidney-shaped
pan. Nightmaring round in

head as in cement mixer, roll-
drumming about to diastole
and systole—off-beats, off-
off-beats.
        To come

out so much sicker than I'd
gone in, fumigations; wake
up at incoherence out-
side, into a chrome-white
surgery, white coats, after

consciousness in the blood and being
bump-turned round through the revolving
doors.

Roll call (Role Call)

      Schoolkids
at the primary school
assembly in adjacent church
hall. Some of the ones
assembled there 'd been caught throwing
stones. Plucked
out of audience onto stage and
meted out punishment with
the strap—hands hardened—cuts'
leather—in wax lemon
or piss. But the rest of us were

impressed. Yonnie fights
were not actually unknown in that
assembly. Not ready—in
spite of the media exposure—to
audition to be an understudy
out there.
          Time's gone,

and gone too the contemporary figures
of authority—canes, straps re-
layed like batons handed on
from headmaster to headmaster—and
finally, too, authority
itself. Nun, soap smells, dark
habit, bleached coif; Christian
Brother's black soutane, small
clerical collar erected stiff
out of underwear—for purity? But

the rest of it is an impure
world. Tact needed
is not just what with authority should

be needed, hardly now *could*
be needed. Stones break
through sealed glass and hurt. Be
shattered again, resealed. Parents

squatting, sitting lawn for school
fete, green stains upon
trouser legs. Gossiping
through decades, chalk, blackboards
are the same, none of the teachers let alone
students. Come
              dark,
switching on of arc lamps around
quadrangle, rows of lights within
classrooms. Night, outside,

wells up in deep springs
of darkness. Sprinkler water flogs
glisten upon the night. Shift, brushing

insects off, loose grass, ants
upon wings, separately from our clothes.

Rhythms to Counter-Rhythms

          Window
rattling on both insides
to a frame —gust-clump, fit-
batterings. Cock further out
crowing, hawk-clearing
the throat, phlegm
               swallow under
recarollings. I repeat myself

in silence not even
a heartbeat can intercept, at
diastole and systole, tread
of a foot walking.

Restoration

Aborigines
had camped inside, cooked food on the pine
floors. With plane and sander
we'd shaved off the burn marks, wood
char. They'd hung billy
from handle by wire slung across forked
sticks—to flames
from firewood split, leaning across
stacked triagonally onto itself
at apex. Then tossed gum twig

on, dimpling water surface—
over which the heat and steam
rose slowly;
            measuring tea leaves
from packet to shake-scatter across
simmer—welling seething up
to a boil.
          Something ugly

had happened, unconnected
with aborigines: it floated
like shadow, like steam off water
surface around twig. One

study had a corner solid
in it, between window
and chimney stack, upright
by a wall. Though the opening 'd been
boarded up, could still slide
air down, yet opened to
no sky—onto blue, the white
clouds. Out in back yard

there were bottle fragments everywhere across
rough ground, at turnoverable
depths, butts and sides com-
pact in clods, compressed
by pressure from the weight of feet
that'd passed there, over space
where once'd been a lawn—times
older than aborigines, seemed
older than the bush. Someone

had lined bottles up against
brick wall of garage, pitched
rocks, fired slug-pellets
from an air rifle t' smash-splinter across
quarter acre block, onto
years. We carefully fossicked
for bits, shivers, larger brown
butts, curved side pieces,
like *objets trouvés* (brown glass—
beer empties, mostly), sifting
hundreds of smaller fragments
at a time, for days,
into months and to years,
before it'd become safe
to walk barefoot there. I wonder whether

the aborigines rented it—told
t' get moving on, whether men
who'd smashed up the empties owned
or rented it? Was this a life
determined on? Been determined
in? Twelve foot

ceilings, pine boards—much
of time hung up there, making our own times
temporary—never been more
than a moment in that place.

              The air blew
down the long corridors just as it had over
a hundred years ago, and nothing
was young then, or now,
                    nor any of us
that'd been living there in between.

The Feast of O-Bon (pron. "Or-Bon") that is, All Souls' Night

for Ian, six years dead

                Bene-
diction on him, blessings on
myself after.

                Gaps gasped

from humidity,
                autumn night
Japan. Crickets through bamboo cages
chirruping in the dark, candles,
tin holders, floated down,
paper boats. Still needing

benedictions from the dead who need
me. Any blessing

is from caves
                under arches
of the bridge, down below
where hollows slide on water, bend
round piles and
                on through arch's
span. Currents cross, criss-
cross in below ripples and
sub-ripple, reflect roll on
to moonlight, dipping dull and bright
to a full moon, but peace is in

the darkness, is the reason
we must regroup. Neons on
the riverfront rotate electric
round black buildings leaning out

reflexion onto water—neons
synchronising in reverse—bulked
at dawn within mist rising, above

handrails wet with dew.

THE "LATE" SECTION FROM
COLD'S DETERMINATIONS

Skywriting

              The monoplane
drift-buzzes across cricket fields
in summer, time stretching out
lengths into long lives
of youth, onto eternities
in smoke, dipping to sign-write
and turn. White
                swells, trails

smudge. Plane smoke-dots,
and drops off, unsigning. Buzzing

on to rear-visible
in sky-blue. Ejaculates
sound, intermissions after
mission, trails silence across

exhaustion, landed, on last in, motoring
on off.

Below the Waterline

        Grounded
see-saw on the butt to jolt
friend up, flying bump-grabs
from other end, spreadeagling
out most directions. Jolted into

air to save, yank clutch-ons,
myself, sliding up-down
broad splinters to get purchase, varying
length of the fulcrum, con-
                      trolled
body weight dumped in on
its saddle.
        Irritating

after timing and mis-
                timing var-
iations to make last bucked
jolt up as if anything
but final. Slipped off dis-

mounting t' climb welded steps
on slide. Slid, legs splayed, grip-
skidding with the feet down tubed
margins. Rockclimbed a way

back up on reverse of slide's
scaffolding; stomach-head-slide; shinning
frog flippers again where
I'd slid.
        Us kids then

shove off, return home, stomach
rumbles to be weighted on
formally (though had been summoned there
for the umpteenth time, sharply none too
friendlily), setting cutlery on
the table, grounded at our back-
sides, pudding's weight off to
contentment.
              Back out into

park past twilight, gathering
of mosquitoes, noise abducted through
sound spaces.

           Red points
in the dark group-materialising
as cigarettes. Talking hulks mutate
family and friends.
              Mozzie

buzz-whines tail off about
ear chamber, abrupted
at anticipations of light touching
on exposed surfaces. Push wire

door open from the back yard,
come in. Spring-closes, grating
at back—night closed out
like reverse of shops' Open signs
on glass doors. We turn round

to hear crickets—sound before
not noticed. Night's darkened
from inside the house, light's switched on
till day.

The Life's Work

                              They
worked with scrubbrush, floor mop, time
of my mother—
                    late as that.
And *soap*, not detergents. Learnt
how t' *use* it—not
                    direct on your face,
never, if not a fool, on your hair:
'You wet it first.' The
                         'properties of soap',
its 'chemical composition', what it 'is'—
what would you want to know it for? Laboratory

scientist working on floor on his knees,
white coat, starched, sleeves roll-folded, avoiding
drag soap through slops on the floor. But you learnt

how to live with it—using the brush,
prick-dip of bristle in oblong bar—what's
the texture?—'as slippery as soap'?
Try this with detergent powder. What

that gives

is a 'function'—different strengths of same thing,
as chemicals, ammonia—who's learnt to live
with *ammonia*?! 'If swallowed,

seek medical advice.'
                      What you get to know
are the aftermaths of such things. I remember

my mother down on her knees
                              with a scrubbing brush,

back arched, then flattening out at scrub-shovings, wisps
and straggles of hair itching face till she'd curved them
back onto fingers after wiping hand across apron. The strength

of the experience nothing to do with the communality
of the material, nothing to do with the fact
she was my mother not my sister (who didn't have one).
Past pasts

're not so real or so
illusory. God knows

the nothings we build onto them, *into* them, of what
consistency or body weight the memory. My mother,
exhausted after gesticulations on a death bed, left me
her bamboo beads for the rosary in a felt case,
and her blessings too,

as substitute for what she
                       hadn't said to me

for what she didn't say—
                       till I never wanted to hear it.

On Bivouac

We dug trenches with spades
on fatigues—had to use crowbars
to break into the clay soil. Didn't
sleep down in them any nights—sliding
winds, open slopes out
off the ridge—erecting tents,
guy ropes pegged out wide to sides
tightened from clouts off wooden hammers.
                                          Gathered

twigs and branches still
left over—
though competed for
as scarce by other companies.
                            Fires

caught by wind, flattened under
pots used for cooking, water
heated for coffee. "Whose
                        pannikin?"
"Not me sarge, I'm
perfectly calm."

And the night calm too, under
no singing
        by campfires:
Bretony, war zone or the Western
Front.

But not
        even adolescents, just
boys.

And the matter sang, crackle-hiss
in outflow from saucepans, alu-
minium with the bonded
lids
     and the shooting to pop-crack
from sparks rising on

up out of mountain heights.

Ex Cathedra in Bourges Cathedral

            Pencilling in
notes on the sextipartite
vaults, gloved hands, listening
to sounds dampened from space volumes
under them. Catching at
trumpet stop of the organ, oboe
metalling by the string courses along
arches. Verger pushes me

aside, and quite irritably,
from cross-aisle to the vestry, clearing
way for bridal procession out of
side door. I sit down

in the pews while the wedding couple
has welded four hands
at crossing before chancel round
altar. The hundred and forty foot

vaults hold them, light descensions
falling like confetti. The bride's
worn fur—it *is* cold. I

construe it: better to marry than
to burn. The Buxtehude

organ prelude floats church
down pointed vault over furs, bestial
on shoulders, white wedding silk
underneath. Cathedral's un-

disturbed, subtends bay height
from the human relativities. I
clap hands, make no echo, then

proceed back of the wedding company, confetti
outside floating light shafts
in sunshine. The black sedans

roll up, reorganising
gravel. I drink black coffee, feet round
struts of bar stool at a bistro
door.

The Effort

We're

ready to try again

with day.

Last Watering Place

Horse
      trough
            set
in concrete outside Sarah Sands
pub—last drinking stop
and watering place for the horses before
Melbourne. Among horse-drawn
vehicles would be brewery drays
themselves, wooden barrels across
large flat trays
to the drays—odd driver carting
gallons of the product in
himself before refilling
out of big vats on returning casks
to the brewery.
            They blasted

horse troughs with pneumatic drills, cracked
concrete legs, boltings as
a traffic hazard, cement broken
like rocks, relaid kerb, re-
tarred the footpath.
            Trucks and semis

stand waiting for the lights to change
at corner where Clydesdales
had clink-clankered harness across
huge shoulders, dropped dung without
least sign of effort under
tails bound tight up at
docks to be lifted clear
of hindquarters—later joining
with community of horses at
the trough like drivers them-

selves inside in
leather aprons, rivulets and
slurpings from their drinkings at the
bar/trough. Not so much

besottedness or chyacking with
the horses. Mafia rule

what's been for long Italian suburb
in Brunswick,
                yet the darkness not
from Androgheda but exhaust pipes
of the massive Mercedes Benz semi-
trailers, cars, sundry commercial
vehicles, fumes settling down
visibly as grime. Suburb
was for factories, workers' houses around
flanks by brick walls, second storey

broken glass windows, ineffective
wire screens. Narrow
streets were for carts, dodging
pedestrians that surrounded, then
veering back to avoid tanglings
from wheels of other carts. The footpaths,
where there *were* any were crowded
but slow, not spaced
for ducking out of parked cars into
shops. Brick buildings stand

still, stone guttering un-
replaced yet by concrete. It looks
not to have aged but's remained
old as the age
itself.
        Fluorescent lights come

on at the Sarah Sands
bar,
     early
in winter. Through panes and blue
leadlight I see heads,
slouch hats, quiffs of hair, semi-
baldings. They take their
ale just as slowly as
beer drawn from barrels for
wearers of leather aprons, that once
rumbled them across footpath to
opened up cellar grates,
                      before bumping them
down in.

Double or Quits

Bouncing echoes off
walls at the dead end
of a street, getting y'r own back ("...ing
y'r own back"). YOU NONG: "...wu-
nong." "PULL Y'R HEAD IN!" "...'ll
y'r head in." Time's foreshortened, rico-
chetted doubled doubling after-
takes.
      As sound

of the kick 'f a football echoes up
through back 'f a stadium split second after
a kick. We played un-
social games, bellowing down
asphalt for the echoes, on to
hollow up to wood palings in
back fence at smaller rise
to the end, green gables of
a garage's rusting corrugated iron
roof. Taunt-shouts would've

driven the owner barmy, pedo-
cidal. "That's how it *is*
with kids"—
        is *not*
what they'd thought. Bellowing back at us
flushed with rage—no echo re-
projecting back to them (we'd tested it
from that slope). But *our* taunts
did for us, surfing back
on peaks and troughs in otherwise
still air. Ghosts of echoes

bounce again from those walls
without a recollection, back in
distances off too far for them

to come.

The Recollection

                    A dog
growl-mouths within meat, grovelling
prayers off till it's eaten, stretches
jaw round dish to worry neat
off, snarling
at interruption, scratch-buries
bone through scrape-mound to
forget it onto decom-
position as humus, scratches up

memory from
under leaf and
                out of earth.

Systole

1

            Easy
way off from me, easy
for me— your easiness
is your own affair—and later.

2.

             Solo
clarinet over drum riff—couples
wade out to rhythms on
a dance floor, pivot, spin, reverse
steps, balancings carried off
from waxed floor polish onto
skirt-air. Comet fluff-flutters

last notes, mash to cymbals. Couples
drop hands, head separately back
to bench spaces, sidle jostling in, talk
separately each with own sex

on their seats.

Family Continuities and Discontinuities

                                        Where
would my grandmother be now, as old woman,
but in her daughter, my mother?—close
on eighty, surviving some years after
the accident that'd nearly killed her—iron
                                        wills

outlasting fatal heart attacks of husbands
and whatever the prior damnation (both men
decently buried,
              dark suits, waistcoats bone-
buttoned down from top, gravediggers
in singlets, trousers with cuffs, shovelling, turning
shovel round to
              scrape earth back in)

so that, left to themselves,

they could be girls again—
              volley railleries:
"You should watch yourself with Mr. Kimberly, the old wolf!", quips
to gentlemen acquaintances at the nursing home—
when passing through—not for-
                            getting their lines,
but no longer
            interested in the plot, even
partners for leg-lock pivotings in the next act.
                                    Mocking
coquetteries (what other sort are there?)
obsolete to all but these men friends (wheeze breaths
coughed up in semi-laughs at such 'stirrings'
by bellows-suction of not much air,
then plunging down for more air as through filters
of a gas mask

        to repeat it).
               My mother

uses a walking stick or dragging stick
for her left side—that would be part-paralysed
if she'd let it. Semi-flinches off a physical
attack not there—but she knows that.
Her own father's straight back, agility through
the prickly would be still there in place,
spite of the crook'd neck. I mean his puritan

and Irish Catholic atheist,
               "flogging sex offenders"

leather thongs in knots across their backs
till winced not with pain but degradation
down to their sex organs.
               Sense he had

of such things: de-
               tumescence, contumescence, chest's
contraction-expansion, sucking whistles in
through teeth clenched from whiplash
across backside's lust-pleasure-pain, sperm
ejaculation from
               jerk-down by gravity
at hanging that was too good for him.
               The old woman'd been

a rollicker in her time, rounded cheeks
                       side
of dimples up from flirt's cleft chin.
               She stole-gathered

flowers at night from graves in the cemetery,
pinning to her bodice with brooch t' wear
dancing at balls of the Scottish Highland

Something-or-others (Caledonian?), spelling her name
the Scottish way not Irish, to get in. What

she *did* at such functions, or
         after,
I never heard from my mother—who'd never heard
herself,
   probably,
       but would've found it
a giggle, at least chuckle, on retrospective—keeping
her puritan nose
       clean from the fun and games—
if there'd *been* fun and games.
         I remember the old woman

dropping false teeth on me; at other times
swivelling eyes to focus off at corners
to me as if an equal—age, experience
not having much to do with it—as if both still
had our lives to live
       that were negotiable:
        love, say,

that had a lot of jokiness in it,
         teasings, a bit
wild and made working class suburbs into
a fairground, pitching-
        in stitched leather shies,
where you got tin whistles for
         whistling throws banged
bang into middle of the leathers between
feathers. Not so much

of this did I realise then,
but *something*—or whether she might've seen
how closed off were all of our poss-
ibilities, that'd always been there,

that'd never not *not*
been there, that'd been there
from the start.
                Not so far

had my mother gone, in this,

nor could. I've watched her unreel, lift
cotton up to the light to thread
a needle, loop pushed through, strands
extruding spread-crushed, tugged
out, twist-secured—gossiping
of past eras, past wildnesses, past
disruptions, later denying within
a readjustable memory she'd
said any of it, *knew*
any of it. That cuckolded (?)

(but I doubt it) labourer husband that
had also been her father, headed back
home of an evening from work, not
to the pub, eating vegetable soup
for dinner, strong back, arms
bare
      down to elbows upon
the table, embracing steam off food
like warmth. While my grandmother, nose
up a bit, picky like
finicky young girl she'd been, stood

by table next to iron wood
cooking stove, shrugging off warm family
as life situation she'd gotten herself
into,
        and made her own.

Mechanical Engineering Show at the Exhibition Building

                People
slide by, like thoughts you don't
press on with. Visitors file

into museum past exhibit of
combustion engine, seeing through
from panel slots how the compression
works.
        Building's walls

are high, plan cruciform over
nineteenth century crossing under
dome; walk wood, sub-
dued by a lack of pace, out through
twenty foot doors anchored

on own weight.

Uses of Iron

            Coulter furrows down
through soil, clods turned over
at the grooves—the rain the cold to
break through in air, make
permeable. The drops fall
continuously 'nd do not wash
away. You put parti-

cularity into lives like
the drops—detach, drain off
through soil, soak in out of
glisten. What does rain

mean to us—seep-in
as metaphor? What
the hell is it metaphor
of? Is it contrast with
earth lump as substantial and
the real?
           We know roughly:

'clear'—as a windbell, rung
iron, shape cast as
a temple bell scaled down, boom
weld, domed ridges at
the sides. Each tinkles

in itself; in carillon, shift
and flutter-twist of clapper cards, through
opening in the storm boards, lift
in breath across night.

Hortus Conclusus

              Turn round
corner on pool
                stagnant at period;
not notice how long water settled, feeling
a lack of shock, you breaking in, undisturbed
surface in the mosquito larvae scum.

Double-storey brick—someone asleep
on top storey, room off railed verandah,
blind not up down
                  long sash window, plaster
arch to keystone: stucco-faced, brick-built
disused convent.
              Someone later

will stroll out through french windows from in creepers
along path among rose beds, near frangipani,
by red rhododendron, shiny dark green
leaf, deeper spines of pines under
light green. The traffic noise lipped

slopped across wall, absorbed
in sea at specific gravity. Mortality
is slowed down, motionless
in dense pool, depth; the green leaves, even
the flowers replaced unnoticeably, and time length
                            stretches beyond breaking

through evening as if be no night,
                      as if
out of the infinity 'd
            be no day.

Retreat in the Jesuit Seminary

To slake thirst, stone lava-
torium, water
getting the job done like a baptismal
font. Medieval fountains,
waters for the monks to wash
hands in before eating
silent in the refectory.
                            Novice

breaths out hagiographies of
a Spanish missionary
                      forced
to eat his own fingers by
Red Indians—practising pronunc-
iation while we eat in silence,
sausages, mashed potato, gravy,
a thin tomato sauce. Over,

chit-chat, subdued, as
we drink coffee, tea—a few,
wine as the medieval monks
themselves would have. Retreat proper,

with vespers in the chapel for
Redemptorist friar resonating onto
pulpit like a soundbox: hell
heaven's by your shoulder—waiting

at the assizes for an interlude
in life itself.
                Night out

on the roof, drags on fags, scoffing
junkfood smuggled in, drinking

beer under bottle like
an udder, watch of stars
through cigarette smoke in skies gone
double, getting a bit peaky
at dawn (making detection more
audible).
        Snuck back

into dormitory to beds. No
warmth yet—eyes open stark—in
blaze of sunlight.
          Back out to

chapel, matins, mass. Mates
pass out from lack of sleep, reeling
over off at incense in

the pews, onto boards down
where we'd been kneeling—otherwise have
puked up and are spirited
away, leaving an odour: "qui tollis
peccata mundi miserere
nobis … dona nobis
pacem … et cum spiritu
tuo": organs, chanting,
off cluster candles in stone wall's

eastern shadow.

Winter Temple

                    Snow
spiralling down among pine trees
on zen enclosure. Street noise
filtered out through wet flakes'

gaps. Had crunched ice
as granita, more snowflakes
settling down like gulls, avoided
skid off glaze's beginnings
on rock, A bell tolled

midday, numbered to syllables
of the Namu Amida Buts(u) linking
centre onto periphery
of ice. A monk walked

from the bronze struck reverberations, clapping
hands both for salutation and
to keep warm, throwing folds' habit
across shoulder, eyeing at sideways
to silence where word greetings would

have been.
           (Perhaps he sleeps on Western
bed in Japanese sliding-door
side room…)
                I gathered thoughts

about me, moving off under
temple gate, my blood warmed
by cold's challenge—yet wanting it
to stop. Later, squat back on heels

at inn, near stove, on raised tatami
mat. The body shivers,
recollecting just how cold it's been

as it's thawed.

Down from the Mountains

Walked over footbridge across
the river, Arashiyama, hearing
shop's amplifier eddying music back
on water from where I came. The noise

dunked, and waterlogged, sub-
marine'd—wind lifted drifting
above it. My own gravity

jerk-walks me down to bank
edge, to crouch over the
side on haunches, lob stone
in, plink-plunk—notes
rolled up as jellied fruit, bobbing
back off it. The pop songs

nasally through from static of
the amplifier are clear but much
diminished in volume ('minume'?). The world's
through the wrong end of a telescope reaching
off further back. Recross macadam

road, purchasing windbells
out of shop stalls, brushing past dangled strips
of plastic, steering off face, by coat
shoulders. The till's ring-sprung-
jerk nudges from hip level
at silence-gap. I watch the long boats

poled off through the mountain sides
that funnel rapids. Like highwire walkers, boatmen
balance sides on flat boat bottoms
from the slips' stream.

Childhood Illness

                Asthma
gasps, duck head down
under cloth t' breathe up
steam out of enamel dish—in,
out to reciprocities
of notion—steam floating from
eucalyptus oil
                emulsion so
wheeze bass can suck in
pure air—chest bellows for
successive efforts to
                breathe a little
easier: lying back on my
bed measuring life out
in short breaths. Winter light

sharpens until afternoon's
withdrawn. Light reflected
on ceiling above roller blind un-
impeded by shadow-shaft or
heat quiver. Clear bright
re-
    tracts, straight lines under-
shadow in blue-grey, purples
de-intensifying. Life lasts

a single day, moth timespans,
out there. Traffic noise, squeals,

shouts of play from park, clearer,
further off. Cold made
visible from in warmth
of the blankets.
              Left to self

as before during cooking
for dinner, audit sounds
from kitchen: saucepans' clatter coll-
isions, noise of scrapings-across,
iron to iron, jerk-joltings
on-off of taps—water
halted; and the winding themselves
up of chimes in
the loungeroom jang-jonging through
the quarters; shock openings of

door onto air
of passageway out of ingress-
egress. Day stops, night

settles in on preparations
for dinner: cabbage steamed off,
potato mashed in milk and butter,
parsley sauce, boiled carrots to
corned beef, gelatinous fat
rind. Yet much too
tired out, by this,
to be eating. Then tucked back

into bed after using
bedpan, within folded clean
sheets, to remake my bed
warm. Back's
                asthma itch
scratched, grooves side
of spine, nails dug deep
(Into lungs preferably): settling down
for the night. Mum's treadle machine,

clothes' repair, rapid stitches—
suction up of catch, sound
non-symmetrical with click fastening it back

on next to needle—mum's
face concentrated above it
in a frown. There was space to breathe

in,
    not induct the air

down.

Legal Access

Ian, myself, others

who knew us, differentiating
the cases—'friends', my friends
or his. After his marriage

"had finally broken up", walked
through park together, cold sunlight,
forest floating sun motes
among trees. Easter—late onto
Autumn—night settling
like undergrowth—clouds clearing up
for a frost. A three-quarter
                              moon
waxing, no waning—blue
deepening down from pale
onto dark. Earlier,

the kids had been on merry-go-rounds,
blurring around, horses' crankshafts
vaulting slow, spaced out
among trees,
            heads clutched at the carved
manes. We ambled away

from kids—off themselves into
gallop rhythms, ticket box for
side-shows, hands slapping back-
side, riding crops across
cruppers, reining mounts in with a
"Whoa there", dis-
                mounting, hitching
horses t' hitching posts, smoothing their
shoulders, flanks down, lurching

through saloon doors into a honkytonk
dance floor; gals, knickers off
for can-can's 'can-
            not', con-
cluding on fracas. Running off a

crouch through plastic tunnel's in-
flationary deflation, awarded
stickers for "Having
a go",
      jostling through at next
turnstile onto chairs of a whirl-
igig, lifting them up to meet
centrifugal force against which they're
strapped in.

      On stage, Irish
folk singers (but that rig's
Irish?!) patter-talk, miming
railway gang laying tracks from the last
century, singing working class
 tunes, 'bog Irish', hornpipes
sound like cheeky whistles to get
y'r skirts up.
      Kids stick close
each to own adult, no
grouping 'cept in play, de-
taching re-attaching him-
me. Whisk off

from our sides to a venture playground's
putlogs, shin commandos up
at risk, just within call
of strollings from our security. Rousings,
shoutings up through fortress as
through amplifier, erupting out in

chuckle-giggles, scramblings against being
spotted, caught. It's already

too cold outside to identify
with sunset beauty, tingling with
a final clarity, premonitions
of a frost.
         All forms

back from the human, deep
in twilight dark, trees, the hedges
solidifying into it. Autumn
dusk's sunlight brush-scrapes
around trees, flicks on elm leaves
in transparency, gold lit
at serrations. I catch
from shadow a leaf move further
back, flash like a swept
handtorch, startlings from a small
sound. What are we meant

to do? This's the only
forever we've got. Not
time itself but the materials
are transitory. Present time,
solid as shafts of sunlight between
trees, shifting motes. Hanker
for no more depths of experience than
I've got, just that whatever
I *do* have fills my capacities
to completion.
         "Life of some
significance"?
         What the hell would that
be? What am I doing
in it? Wind gusts

buffet, eddy, floating kids'
shrieks, lift them high up
to vaulting among trees. Side-

shuffle-skips, scuff-rushes
thud pavement back to angle-parked
car under street lights, go
brawling in through opened door,
elbowing room to shoulder-jamming
over-jostled complaints to bounce
up cushions wedged in on the back
seat. Gear changes,

diverging home back way by the side
streets, clickings up-down
of indicators. Returned. Unbutton
key wallet to shake out door
keys, scratchings into lock, then
bursting into hall space like
a drug raid, overcrowd the lounge
furniture, adjusting body spaces
together. Yap-squeals, half-

choked laughter behind preparations
for dinner, heat in and out of
kitchen, laughter, movements
through pockets of cold. Sit around

table, re-stirring waves
in choppy ripple-chuckle. And night,
and time for sleep,
                    till they come,
or they go.

Storage Space

              Wandering
at the back of old shops, down
lanes cobbled the same time
last century. Visiting students then
I knew—

            George South, splitting
wood on axe effortlessly
in one hand; hovering over,
stoking up the fire using
poker, —by its end shift-levering
logs off to allow it
draw air.

            Camped down
in house like campsite
for gypsies, chock wedges
under caravan wheels to stop
rolling, steps lowered under
pitched roof.

            Only flames flaring
out of splittings in the wood lit
the room—lathe and plaster up to
picture rail no frames, now that
the Heidelberg School prints George
'd jerked off had been put out
for storage with lumber in the back
shed. Late Victorian, too,

the house, yard, lane, even
the suburbs, and as far away from us
then as those discussions into the
wee hours of the morning thirty

years ago are remote from us
now. And George, too, only

a year later, in ground floor
rented flat, cast iron
railings out by steps down
to the basement, met head-on by
himself some problem over
his right to live and took his own

life, putting his head into
a gas oven, closing its door back
in upon himself, turning
the jets on. I never saw

the flat, nor learnt
what year, model, brand had been
the gas oven, stamped
in letters onto its cast-iron
door, what precisely by the
tape measure were the dimensions
of the area.   My friend anyhow
had gone, gone whiff
of the gas that had asphyxiated
and killed him, by any time
I could've gotten there. Thirty years

on, his absence isolable
as all events then. I will bury
any memories in repository
with myself, to retain as reliquaries
of them all.

Off and Out

                Fly
zigzags in run-scuttle
across garbage. Rub-scratches its
forelegs to itch-equivalent
of flies. Lays, hatches out

eggs on meat storage
for larvae. Seems to take time

off to loll through its one
day. In sun warmth, goes

earthed spark winging dark mote
through brightness,
                          smudges buzzing across
burial grounds, untouched future
years.

The Wreath

                         I'd
skewered the frog with pitchfork to
scare it off, cleaned it from
the fork, shovel-burying into
shallow grave. The fear was

on me as it twitched, reflex
action or alive still with
a prong in it? Put a row

of spuds in there later, tubers
covered over in layers
of earth. Picked-unearthed them after
growth, jumbling handfuls I had
picked. With a knife point scraped
eyes out, after paring loops
of peel off. The frog grave

was as sacred to the earth as
earth itself is to
our sustenance from it. It squatted

quiet, made no statement
of its death, topple-sank with
the spadework turning earth over where
it mouldered.
               Stakes suspend

green peas, string bean in
tendrils
       over the clods where
it lay.

Past Futures

The sort of school

gone—that I was educated
in.
Nostalgia? Not

for anything in the past, but
future never was, never
will be.
        Factory grime

in buildings round quadrangle
of red brick. Drinking taps
out in playgrounds above curved grates
to the gully traps, pieces from
cement base chunked off
convex or concave concrete
walls. And us, drinking there
in the queues, mouths to taps, off,
lines squirted, spraying wild
jets around, fingers into
bulb holes, the back-spray slip-
wetting own shirts faces
hair. And bump-contests, hoppo-
bumpo, lumbering piggy-back,
siege towers to enclosure, double-
tiered for Release of
prisoners who'd release you
in their stead. Recess ends

on school bell's ring-clunk
from soundings of crack-fault
in the metal, or with resonance
from unfaulty bell circling round own

sides like an auditorium throwing
hums off lipped metal
of the bell. Blood kick-started to

life for next period
in the classroom, jerk-vaulted on
up a bit higher
than the tasks. All quietening down

to scuffle-settle in desks. Work
copied off from chalk writing
on blackboard—into exercise books
pressed down, the pages turned
in unprefabricated
silence. What then

did we learn?
                Nothing much
for out of school. Out there
was a universe of work, tasks
full as lives—variety bringing
possibilities of disruption
to all this—as with the pumped blood
of playtime.
                Many worlds still

opened for us out there: baker,
bread van, creaking wheels, snort
of horses;
                milkie clink-clunking
bottles in first twilight
of morning, open cart, small
wheels, rubber tyres, horse,
horseshoes' iron flush-clops
on road metal. Grocer, groceress

corner shop, white aprons, needle
scales. The bottle-o carolling
"Any old bones or bottles?" What he
was, surly, twisted like
a knot of wood in the grain
of our lives. All out there, ready
to be taken on, still the possibilities

to be lived.

Cold's Determinations

                Too tired
to breathe, gasp in air out
of reflex, to laze in death
coma, settling down
to an authority that is not mine, any
of whose control would be relative
to this absolute. My father dozed off

over wood stove fire within
kitchen—back wall flue—getting
warmth in against other chills
out of death.   Delayed leaving
to go out to the bedroom or
set alight slow wood
combustion fire t' shift chill off
the lounge where room temperature'd
only gradually warm up. He died

finally, outside visiting hours,
by himself in the Royal Melbourne
Hospital—sheets fastened
across chest, tight-secured
under mattress within a mitre
tuck. Ward—returning—contained

no physical evidence
of his being there, or traces
of specific illnesses to other patients
from the past.   Doors opening

out of lift onto Casualty
Ward—as before except

for distribution and spread
of the patients. Same chills
off draughts from wheelchair ramps
under doors. My brother

filled in the standard forms
for an autopsy, while my mother kept
repeating to herself
that he was young—only the tone used
putting question to the rest of us
was it right? What after all

is the proper length of a life? Does
the specific length give measure
of some meaning? Not too much

meaning in my own life that

a death then or a life now
leaves unsettled, or would've confirmed either
positively or negatively as
unlikely to have been true.

POSTSCRIPT

A Need for Manipulation

                Pain
in the neck, crick, open current
across brow, rub press, stroke,

firm cranium to neck structure
at pause—block-
                head. With a

"lack of concentration"
you couch floor to forehead, medi-
tate holding root brain
from shift, off core, something
to live with
                centred on
something to

            live for.

Post-Obituaries

Whom
do I talk to instead of my
dead friends?

Would they still listen?
Say much the same thing?

Would time
stop for our talks? No

luck with their presence,
and their absence if it had
to be that should've been
final.

       Need

to be free of their memory
if memory's all
we're to have. I did not
ask for such loss,
nor for the necessity
to live with it. Would

it were ununderstandable—as if
I never knew them—people out of last
century. Consequently,

we've tossed out years
as you toss out old calendars.
                    I look around

for the places we've been

but no longer know where to look for them.

The Avenue of Trees

Why pause? Never to start
again? Clouds pile up,

gather on wind, different
pacing from the spiralling
among leaves, dry-scrape
over concrete. I am at a loss

for ideas because at this age
I want to be—though plenty
around, drag-swept
off the path, leaves piled up
at edge to be mulched. Better

winter should stay litter-
free, through bare branches
of plane trees—melodies,
no harmony—
                    turquoise
sunsets; after,

a frost blue.

Match Points

      The sound of
a ball against wall on
tram sheds—pinged gut, doubling
echoes off brick corners
of the sheds. Yet fifty years on,

I return sound, stroking echo
in echo, staying outside
of time as I did then, blocking
volleys back, racket
or no racket.

          Have no attribute
to endure, am the nothing
that anything's past substance
'd be among. No memory's left

of a self, or a recall
in others. No silence forms

as the negative t' return endings
from.

Long Division

Times numberable.

Make sure you get the calculation
right.

So you are left with number—

to number number.

              All recollection

intact when you open it.

To hold up to the light—test your eyes
for "what it must have been".
Do we remember
"what must have been" and what we saw, as separate?

The world is what it is.
Our record of it
likewise and verified, "simulacra",
replicas of what we think, and not
"the other"—if that is anything.

            I can count instances
of time as I count, toes, but can't repeat
the counting.

         Pain/pleasure
numberable too, like other events—
         granted, when to begin and stop —

so we are left with number—

that counts itself.

A Day Off

        The people
don't mean much—they never did—
                I always wanted them
to mean something—provided it worked out
            when we'd get together—
what we are, what we could be,
      and the two were arguably related. We'd go back

to what we thought we had in common—but
out of sight's out of mind—you think that's only
for a time, but time's all we've got,
not much left over for passing it with our friends.

We find out how they are occasionally, get involved
sometimes with their problems, if handleable,
trot out advice, pass back to them
in silence if they're not—the prostate cancer?
Let's hope there'll be no metastasis.
                    We brush up against them

in the street: it's our day off, promise to keep in touch—
                but who's the one
we'd keep in touch with? Yet—
good to have the contact, hands shaken,
hug, brushed cheeks if a woman. But,
we must be off—
          wave as we turn to go.

A Buzz out of the Regiment

The flies at Pukkha clung to cracked
lips, working them into sores. We'd
try to blow them off, over-
under lipping fluffs, but they'd
resettle, when'd ever bothered
t' shift—buzz-clump. Right

turn to march off mo-
mentarily disturbs them—not
as much as settling would've disturbed
us—parade ground
in the heat. Some solace to

be At Ease, but you couldn't raise
your hand to brush them off—and the flies

knew it.

Individuals in Collectivity

                    Small
ant shouldering bread crumb
twice the size, breaks out
in trot, goosesteps on all
legs.
      Over road, ants

file across caterpillar un-
folding rolls in transit, take
bites one-by-one off
its back. But…
living meat, ignoring
dead grub part-eaten, two feet
short of road border
it'd dragged towards.
                Dawn,

ant particulars, confused, twitch
feelers before deviation, stop,
barge-start, stop,
              going

solo in the frost.

Returnings

                        My
"memories lost"? Unverifiable
by dead friends or my brother. Sort,
to slip them into place just
where they were. But places now
're dispersed that once we'd been
embedded in. I would
embrace a death if bodies too
could be reunited and sites preserved
in which so much of our lives
had been passed.
                No
                    such

luck. They come back to us

in dreams, like light shafts di-
agonal with the opening
of a door, sub-
            dazzle un-
affected by death, not now
much interested in it, left to another
time. I visit them—

haven't kept up contact for many
years—still renting a place
a neighbour cleans
who waits on the doorstep for them.

Low Tide

      1.

          Clumps
of ti-tree. Towels rumpled, left
after insulating bodies over
the sand.

       Three youths, one
a girl, laughing, wade-lurch
through water, dip for splash-fights,
with shrieks, shouts, edge
of the surf, low tide. Bay

curves back to headland
on right—hull
in dry dock; bluff
to the left. White clouds
                puff
across, interrupting
the sunshine oc-
casionally, fluffs to a cool
breeze. I wouldn't know

what age I am, nor them, nor from
what age. The bathing suits cut
up and away at the thighs to clutch
crotch, but the youngsters' play
is half-asexual. Roars
from sand and tide 're low but are
extensive. The wash rocks
in choppy ripples out swelling
its contours. Checked further off
still, and waterlogged, be-
calmed down to the depths
of the ocean.

2.

The past

is another country—and I'm

not living there.

Burning of the Great Dai* on Daimonji

On fire, Dai, top of the hill,
smoke drifts off
                dead souls to the North, dog days of summer.
A crowd, nearly the whole population, watching it,
as they'd watched the fireworks, a month earlier,
on the banks of Arashiyama, when Alison passed water
to signal how close labour, was given a lift
by anonymous Japanese, and that night, later,
in an obstetrics ward of the Japan Baptist Hospital,
gave birth to her first-born—Siegfried—

and mine.

A Sino-Japanese ideograph meaning "great".

Training Route

for Ron Stewart

Distance off in time—a jog-jerk run,
pants by the barbed wire fence; stretch it wide,
hand and foot to let each other through,
dodging the flicking barbs; straightening, escape
gingerly along ploughed ridges, furrows, cross
to side of paddock opposite, stretch again
slack wire, minding the rusted barbs, out
across slope past aerodrome at Essendon,
creek detour (swollen in wet season) down through contours
of what had once been riverbank. Refill lungs,
gulp-gasping air; decide to turn back home,
near limping with the tiredness, unsettled strides to pound
down slopes, knees wobble-jerked in stress
uphill. Then back home, stop off for a drink

near Ron's place at milk bar on the corner,
sold flavoured milk in pints, chocolate, strawberry—
cheaper than either milkshake or the malteds,
not thickened with froth, like such, off scoops of ice cream,
"The Health Food of a Nation" (brand was Peter's).

We'd talk over the universe—head, lungs
trying to draw in air, gasp out words,
though I can't remember *anything* was said
(thank God), but what it meant—we were young,
the world wide, us breathing in it, *that*
I do remember—knew it then. The rest?
With me still. But youth and its activities?—
milkshake without the malt? Long time ago.
Some of the houses remain there yet, stranded
in a world that's not their own. I see them there

and keep them there, in a former everyday:
weatherboard, unrenovated—as they were.

Hygiene

      Dead
bird on back,
wing half-spread
        head
lolling on side.
Ants
filing to/from wound, cleaning
it up.

Some Sense from It

              Either
you die when you grow old, or everyone
else does.

I'm confused at the speed
it's happened, and the stealth
of the replacement. Did anyone give us
notice? Looking the place over,

to see if it makes sense, could
again;
        or
re-enact the time in a land that is now
alien.

Manipulative Crafts

                    Friends
are gone. When do I talk to? You?
My enemy? I listened once
to all that friends said—who told me

near everything. No need

to say it now, for you are no friend
of mine, not even my friends' friend.

                I have no further use
for myself, such as they did.
                          Bunraku

puppet on stage, jerky with anger,
gloved, worked by the puppeteer, unhooded face,

dark robe
within the brocade costumes.

The Fifty Year Reunion

                Slide
back without interruption, here we are
young again? Ageing's made no difference?
Or events between?—marriage, employment, bringing up
kids: who leave home, go
off by themselves (and from us)? While we're at this time-refuge left over
in old age like the survivors
of an earthquake. And the volcano rumbled, houses gone,
parents, friends still walking above ground
in youth, places we knew,
all compacted, preserved
under the lava. And it happened

at night, us safe in bed, feeling only
the heat and stench. Ours was not even the same
earthquake. Not nostalgia, either, any of us

feels, but con-science, to know what
we know, how little that is and nothing more.
We search for the old humour, give ourselves
a break —
          stabilise
in a now as if a back-then-that-we-knew;
but the Then is anywhere, viz. nowhere; and we've only had
occasional experience in it—of events themselves,
or of the times during which we were present at them.

Marist Brothers' College Bendigo

Still there—if further off than it was—
    no longer within coo-ee—my primary school

days at the Marist Brothers',
                  Bendigo,
where a fat man, belly bulging
under waistcoat, buttons stretched out
to pop, gave speech
to the whole school assembly: "…this
fat man spoke…" and the kids
coughed, spewed up laughs. I remember

injustice done—head remote
in high school, me primary,
had blitz on latecomers, frosty morning
in May. I was late for the first time
that year. Head-eye in-
dications to detach myself
ranks outside primary school,
stumbling off unco-ordinated,
catch the breath, to sixth form,
front of the men in desks. Dealt
six strokes from a cane, swishings
to each hand, which swelled up so
badly it disabled me
from holding pen till midday, nor
forced to by class teacher
though a strict disciplinarian.
And my hands hung loose like baseball mitts. Sharp

now as it was those fifty years
ago—
and the time
will go with me as I with it. Not

temporary our stay, it remains
unaltered. Not permanent,

either, as each bobs to cascade in silence—
                      roars from the river.

Serial Modes

                    Live life
to the full? I want to live life
to the empty. There's nothing
to fear—

spiralling off into memory,

avoided within a void.

Substantial Identities

Old age lacks the duties,
working to keep a job. No point,
purpose doing things sooner or later.
You c'n wear with not doing them at all.

Anxiety that you might be found out
as a fraud—for that's what you are:
impersonating identity they thought you had,
and *that* you had—to keep up the pretence.
And "Know oneself"? What self that would know oneself?

It has not aged, hanging always about with us.
Should we hear what it has to say, look into the matter?.
Or wait for people to care, see if they recognise *any* of us?

Nobody Home

           The levels
of despair: I've had it quiet
some time now: footnotes,
no text, stories, no one's
interested if they're told. End?
Who'd care? or whether there'd ever been
a beginning. No one home

at my place—never was—
you're not invited. Look "within"—
                              find
Nothing there? No, quite a lot:
constriction about the heart, wheeze
from lungs, liver bulge
(what that would mean), lack of interest
in going on.

           Do I stir

again from shadow, re-
                 search,
opening up the spaces
in blank? opening blank
between the spaces? Where would movement
be from, to? What freedom's left

to despair?

Exchange between Acceptance and Recalcitrance

        1

"You feel depressed?"
                "They've changed the word, despair's
more like it—
        so watch your language."

        2

            "It takes some cheek

to think we'd have it right for the very first time—

and that our opinions—or us—should last for ever."

Gesticulating with Whalen in the Open Air

Phil, burly man like Dr Johnson,
rolling Amerirish accent, rock-
lapping to pre-laughter, strolling Kyoto's alleyways
like thoroughfares cleared to dawdle.
                                      Pontificating
in jest, but listening too. I never knew
the thin Buddhist monk
                        but he'd have known everyone.

Ave atque vale, Owen Faust

Boy soprano lilts
"Cherry ripe, Cherry ripe
Ripe, I cry", tilts
stage barrow to ground shafts,
lean elbow on triangularly
at the tilt, wears a Tyrolean
hat, black mustachio, boy
smile on the lips to mix
nations.
   Deeper voice emerging
later as my protective elder
brother, rapid responses to
a bullying—explanations
demanded not taken. Bully
cuffed but submissive
to the cuff. Arguing "Arts

and Sciences" with his ignorant younger
brother, driving their mother "mad",
from recollections shot
with silences of her own parents and
squabbles about a brother—
who drank. "Don't worry
your mother", dad said—sit-
uation gotten out of her
control. We could've rattled on,
bad argument niggling bad arguments
for ever. And, as a mature man

(I missed most of his youth), teaching
startling science tricks in North
Borneo, founding a teachers' college
to coach local science teachers
teach startling tricks. A long way

back those times,
all times—so is he—re-
collected by the only one
to survive it now—
                    viz. me.

Dusk from Inside the House

Daylight's left off, shrunken inside—almost
gone;
       twitter flitters across branches
through air eddies.
               Night's come in, faded on; I'm
to rest with it—at shadow deeper
than dusk. I blunder into dark
in the next room, leaving it almost
too long—my eye cannot pick out objects. Find corner
to huddle in. Day keeps track

of itself—lifts off, blue-grey
through orange ridges. It
               knows it will be back,
but not for
        a very long while. I sit on haunches with
forever—take my time

to understand it.

Collapsions

Age
drags time together.
You know it was much like this
often, when you were young,
endurance cramped then stretched beyond breaking point,
hoping for any event to intercede
so life should not be extended, for so long, that,
when not buoyed up by your jockstraps at sex
times'd be as unusable as now,
if not,
      as now,
            collapsing on the moment.
            My dead friends,

few living ones, are scattered, isolated,
not in touch; keep modestly polite
through what we'd all have jeered at, cocked leg/snook at
when we were young, conforming to the young,
not to the aged—that'd now be us—
with platitudes of whatever group we're members of.

I don't want much from youth, would want that,
my "lip" back —if I'd imagine getting it
(or anything else). And to have my friends—women even—
rescued from the past to hang around
so death stopped still, or took a breather
(perhaps sometimes it did),

and speculation itself to be less dark,
so that
out of the hours from midnight I could

conjure up day.

Corollary to a Theme of Corman

Let out a fart, another takes its place.
Breathe out only that you can breathe in again.

There's nothing left to get rid of this emptiness.

Out to Do Some Shopping

Silence unshifted
the motorbike trails across—engine
revs up through gears, twists
t' the throttle. Silence reclosing
in, no meaning
vocal on it. Horizons

gather—wet trees
dark in winter. No flight
to it, from it, across through it. Speech
trapped in at other me's
you don't know. Dense with acceptance

will be anything that's said, no matter
the I that listens is never the I
that speaks. Not even
to itself?—then why the hell
should it listen? No one else
within call—tossing words hand-
to-hand for the courtesies, like
"How are you?" "Have a nice
day" issued in voucher receipts
at the checkout. I look round

for life as I once looked around
for love. Hopeless. The rain comes
down into carpark
through unclosed gaps
between roof sections.

                    Attendant rounds up

stray trolleys about the parking lot, crash-telescopes

them in.

Route to the Abattoirs

                  Grazed
out in far paddocks
to put some meat on, slaughtered,
or fattened up so they could tip
the scales then prodded up ramps
stumbling over forehooves
                        to be
trucked off to the abattoirs. Herded
through yards into pens pissing,
stinking with fear
                from
smelling death to have
their throats cut, be poleaxed
at the forehead. Nose searches

through other smells, offal in wheeled
tubs shoved along, front of
stomach bulge stretched over
by singlet, splattered offal stains. Nose
in under below stink
for powdered blood and bone smell, not
quite reaching to it. The Maribyrnong

river, thick as mercury, rainbow
sludge in fats. I sometimes got
to go to the river for
a breath of air, ruminate
on its banks.

        The herd moves
slowly through the slaughter sheds
like trucks 've been freighted in on,
but death comes quickly
to members of the herd, carcasses

jolted t' buckling, not yet
neat. The cleavers, after,

separate off bone sections,
from the joint, haunches hung
to be hacked out at retail into
cuts of neat.
          The slaughtermen,

bulked from a staple beef
diet, queue for pay packets
in solid tread, spaced along
through the queue.

Syllables to and from Cid

I hear y' call—is that beyond the grave?
"Beyond" you don't believe in—nor I—
to send a call so far as that: we hope,

despair we hope, in gustings across the wind.

Electric Razor's Somatics

The bristle slips and slides under razor,
soft with age, with air, air white
through bristle, makes grey overall,
white misted into pigment, colour of death, death come up

close. You slip beneath it, strands under a razor,
slackening, non-resistant to the cutting edges.

Closed Discussions with Cid

You argued against God. I argued Gods
against you. You saw "the facts"
scattered with name tags on across whatever is
and us. You had a point. And wanted boldness

with clarity—no subterfuge for ourselves—
whoever that is. To look at death
close up as blank, as switched off lights,
whether or not we have enough batteries
to flash a torch on that dark. You wanted bravery.

Good stuff. Some have it, some don't.
I suspect you did—talked yourself into it
when not needing to. I've no idea
how I would front that test—I'll put it off
if I can. But death's success rate
is enviable. Now it's got you.
That's not a death I've faced too well.
                                              Hangs around,

won't clear off till I clear off with it. Let

you go before it's let go of me.

Foyer

        Hanging around
in death, audience room, hall
height. Solo, been long
time ago. I will stay
here by myself
for ever.
      Noises outside

wall, children laughing, scooters
burr-swish ball bearings rolling
past, tread of feet
cross gravel, onto dirt.
            It has
little to do with everything that is
me.
   It has

nothing to do with anything that is
me.